Amazing Journeys

Living Hope
Christian Center
Madras, OR

Published in Beaverton, Oregon, by Good Catch Publishing.
www.goodcatchpublishing.com
V1.1

Printed in the United States of America

Table of Contents

The book you are about to read is a compilation of
authentic life stories.
All the facts are true, all the events are real.
These storytellers have dealt with crisis, tragedy, abuse
and neglect and have shared their most private moments,
mess-ups and hang-ups in order for others to learn
and grow from them.
In order to protect the identities of those involved in their
pasts, the names of some storytellers have been
withheld or changed.

Acknowledgements

When a book of this nature is assembled, it obviously requires the efforts of many people determined to create, cooperate and work with great diligence. The team from Living Hope Christian Center and Good Catch Publishing were a powerful combination. Darlene Crowley embraced the task of the onsite project manager with passion. Her love for books and the good news these changed lives proclaim were always evident in her work. In spite of the tremendous hardship she faced with her husband, Dan's health and having to run her own bookstore, she pressed on until GCP's turn came to bring the project to the finish line. Darlene, thank you for the diligence, care and love you gave this project. Special heartfelt appreciation goes to all those writers in Madras who worked and reworked, contributing hundreds of hours to this manuscript. Their work significantly contributed to this final product. An equally special thanks to Joe Seitz for his masterful cover art and Vicki Strickland for her amazing photography, who together made this book look as good as it reads.

Thank you Melanie Widmer for your beautifully written story, *Losing a Child.*

Fred Davis of Good Catch Publishing consulted this project. Fred, your love, grace and Christ-like manner never left during the most stressful moments of the adventure. This project would not have happened without your great heart and expertise. Thank you!

The fine team at Good Catch Publishing performed at the high level we have come to expect. Thank you Fred Davis, Peggy Thompson, Melody Davis, Rick Drebert and Maryl Smith. You all delivered excellence again.

Pastor Lee McCloud, thank you for giving us the opportunity to hear these amazing stories. Your desire to show the depth of transformation in the lives of these people demonstrates your faith in others and the work that God does. Obviously, your work has been effective in Madras. We are proud to know you.

Finally, we thank the Lord for the unbelievable work He has done in these lives. What an amazing God!

Daren Lindley
President of Good Catch Publishing
Beaverton, Oregon

Foreword

In a world inundated with dramatization, we often wonder about the stories we hear in the media. Occasionally, when we investigate, it appears the media has exaggerated or enhanced the story for effect. While the story may be engaging or exciting, the depth of impact is greatly reduced when we realize, "It just wasn't so."

In the book you are about to read the stories have not been adapted, dramatized, exaggerated or inflated. They are the real stories of people from right here in Jefferson County. If you were to walk up and shake the hand of one of these people, you would not be star-struck. They are common people. However, the stories of often-heroic proportions show the depth of these still waters. These people have endured some of the toughest moments life can dish out. Sometimes raw, humbling and even heart-wrenching, they are above all 100 percent true. No one polished their image as they sought to maintain their reputation. Rather, the sorrow, pain and tragedy only enhanced the contrast of transformation that occurred.

We know these people and have lived with them in close proximity for years. We can vouch for their authenticity. Now, let's get to know some of our neighbors, some of the most remarkable people you have ever met.

Lee McCloud
Pastor of Living Hope Christian Center
Madras, Oregon

Forgiving My Brother's Murderer

Cindy Devore's story
as told by Peggy Thompson

The boy made sure he stayed in the shadows alongside the house as he quietly moved toward the back door. He walked up the two cement steps and paused briefly outside the door, eyeing the open space where a windowpane had long ago been broken. Slowly, very carefully, he lifted the gun and pointed the barrel through the hole where the glass had been. With his finger on the trigger, he shouted into the house, "Out of the way, Mom! I'm going to kill him!"

Inside a mug of coffee was tipped over and silverware clanged to the floor as Don jumped to his feet.

"Curtis!" his mother screamed. "No!" She was sitting in a chair that faced the door and Don had been sitting beside her. She saw the barrel of the gun.

Curtis pulled the trigger as he watched Don turn and start to run out of the kitchen. Thunk! Nothing happened.

With a sob, the young boy screamed, "It jammed! Oh my God, the bullet jammed!"

He lowered the gun, turned away from the door and slumped down onto one of the steps, where he sat and started to sob hysterically.

The front door to the house was open, and with a quick glance, Mom knew Don had taken off. Running to the back door, she yanked it open, her gaze coming to rest on the crumpled body of her sobbing son. She was trembling violently, and nerves all over her body twitched as the full force of what he had just tried to do overcame her.

Mom struggled to get her son up onto his feet and into the house. "Curtis! Curtis! Come in the house!" She reached out and took the gun from him.

With resignation and despair, he allowed his mother

to help him into the house. She steered him to a kitchen chair where he sagged, put his arms down on the table and lay his head on them with a groan.

"Oh, no. Oh, no."

"Son! Please! What's going on?"

"It's Don, Mom," he said in a voice hoarse from crying.

"What about Don?" She stood by his chair trembling as she gently stroked his hair, trying to calm him.

Curtis took a deep breath, and as he absorbed his mother's loving touch, he poured out his pent-up secret. He told her the vile story of how Don, a friend of the family, had been molesting him for the past year. It all started when Curtis was 13.

"I just wanted to get him out of our house, Mom. I couldn't stand having him in our house and I couldn't stand having him around you. Then I realized that I wanted to kill him! I tried, Mom! I tried to do it!"

When Mom got Curtis calmed down as much as she could, they talked together in low tones for a while. Afterward, she got up and walked over to the kitchen sink where she stood quietly looking out the window. The gun in her hand felt cold, deadly, evil, and she laid it carefully on the sink. Subconsciously, she wiped her hand on her jeans. It was getting dark outside, but you couldn't see the moon yet. Crickets were chirping their night song and the air was heavy with the fragrance of lilacs. Turning to her son she said, "We have to tell the police."

"No! Mom, please! Don't tell the police!" he begged.

She turned to face him and saw stark terror in his gaze. "Son, I know you're concerned about what you might have to go through with the police, but..."

"Don't tell them! Just don't!" he pleaded, hands clasped together between his knees. He wouldn't tell her that he feared much more than the police.

"Curtis, I'm your mother. We have to tell them." So she called.

It wasn't until the following morning that my mom called me.

"Cindy, the police came and took Curtis for a ride. They've been gone quite a while."

The baby was clinging to my leg as I tried talking to my mother. "Just a minute, Mom."

Reaching down for the baby, I picked her up and put her in the highchair. Quickly sprinkling some Cheerios from the box onto the tray of the chair, I picked up the phone again. "What do you mean 'the police' have taken Curtis for a ride? All we have in Blue Lake is a police chief."

Mom started crying. "That's what I meant. I called Chief Randall last night and he came to the house about two hours ago and picked your brother up. He told me he was going to take him for a ride and talk to him."

My adrenalin had started pumping. Brushing my wispy bangs out of my eyes with the back of one hand, I snapped, "Will you calm down? I can't understand most of what you're saying! Start over at the beginning!"

As I listened, I found myself clinging to every word she was telling me. Leaning on the kitchen sink, I was bent over at the elbows with one arm and hand supporting my head and the other holding the phone tightly against my ear. After she finished telling me, I groaned into the receiver, "Oh my God, Mom."

Forgiving My Brother's Murderer

"Oh, Cindy, I have to go! They just pulled up out front. I'll call you back."

Hanging up the phone, I reached for my "smiley face" mug, went to the stove and poured myself a steaming cup of freshly brewed coffee. Inhaling the nutty aroma, I pulled a chair out from the kitchen table and sat down. After first blowing on the coffee a few times, I took a sip while I tried to process what my mom had just told me.

When she called me back she said, "Chief Randall just left. He said Curtis denied everything. Curtis said nothing happened. I don't know what to think."

"If Curtis tried to shoot Don," I began, "you can be sure something serious is going on, Mom. Do you think he'll talk to me?"

"I don't know."

"Well, let's give him a few days. He drops by my place pretty often. Maybe he'll come by and want to talk."

A few days later, Curtis came by my house. He liked to watch TV and play with my kids. I was 16, a full-blown alcoholic, and living on my own with my two children. My mom didn't let Curtis know that she told me what had happened, so I felt I should wait for him to bring it up. Later in my life, I would be haunted by my inability to read the whispered plea for help that was etched on his facial features. Shortly after 10 p.m. he left to walk home. It was almost 11 p.m. when my mother called.

"It's about time for Curtis to come home, don't you think? You guys need to get some rest."

Feeling surprised and suddenly very alert, I said, "Mom, Curtis left for home about an hour ago."

Neither of us would give voice to our growing concern as we went outside our respective homes and looked around for him. We thought he might be sitting on the curb, throwing rocks into the brush, somehow idling away his time as boys do. Clutching my chenille bathrobe close to my body, I doused my front porch light so I could see better in the dark and stepped outside onto the porch. Softly, very quietly, I called, "Curtis." No answer. I looked up and down the road without success, so I took a tour around the outside of my house, calling his name a little louder. "Curtis!"

As fear started to knot in my belly, I hardly took notice of the fact that I had stepped in a puddle of water from the hose. It was still running in the yard, and my slippers had soaked up the water like a sponge.

Curtis had vanished!

Our strong feeling that something was very wrong was reinforced by the fact that after my brother told my mom what Don had done to him, he stuck very close to home. The only places he went, if he left home at all, were my house and a little store across the street.

All of us — Mom, Don, the police station and I — were situated on the same road. Mom and Don lived on one side of the road, several houses apart, and I lived on the other side, within view of both of their houses. Also, the police station was on my side, but down the road a few blocks. If Don was keeping his eye on Curtis, as we began to suspect, it wasn't a difficult thing for him to do, under the circumstances.

The next day, when my brother still didn't come home, we knew beyond a shadow of a doubt that something bad had happened. We feared the worst.

"Mom, Don must have been waiting for him last

night to come out of my house and start walking home."
Immediately, we started tacking up "Missing Person"
posters. We walked miles and miles and tacked them up
wherever we could find a spot.

A stranger was walking close by and I followed my
impulse to approach him. "Here." I handed him a
poster. "This is my brother. Have you seen him?"

He studied the picture for a moment and then said,
"No, I don't remember ever seeing him." He started to
give me back the poster.

I shook my head. "No, you keep it. Would you
please give it to someone else and ask if they have seen
him? Oh, and if anyone has any information at all,
please tell them to call the number on the bottom." For
emphasis, I pointed it out to him.

As I tacked up another poster, I thought about how
we had never considered Don a dangerous person. He
had been a family friend for a long time. We knew he
was a marijuana grower, but half of Humboldt County
was involved in that. As far as we knew, everything had
always been fine. Based on what Curtis had told my
mom, however, we believed down deep inside that Don
was responsible for my brother's disappearance. We just
didn't have any proof.

We started questioning some things. One was that
two-hour drive with Police Chief Randall, after which
we were told Curtis denied everything.

Another thing got our attention. As soon as the posters went up, the media flooded our small town and
started asking questions. The police chief told them,
"We have had several sightings of this young man. He's
considered a runaway."

On the phone, I said, "Mom, did you hear what Chief

Randall had to say about Curtis? That he's a runaway?"

"That's absolutely not true! Your brother stuck close to home. He was afraid to wander."

Again, after Mom filed molestation charges, we learned that Don had never been questioned by the authorities nor had they initiated a search for Curtis. More fodder was added to the fire when Chief Randall quit his job and moved out of state about four weeks after my brother went missing. That's when we found out that the police chief and Don were good friends.

"Mom, this definitely has a stink to it. When you add all these things together, it looks like Don's police friend did his best to cover up Curtis' disappearance."

"Do you think he found Curtis... the body... " She stuffed her fist in her mouth to keep from crying out.

"All I know, Mom, is that this hasn't been handled properly." I sat brooding for a few moments. "They probably thought, 'What's one more dead Indian?'"

Mom gasped as I alluded to our Native American culture in such a derogatory way.

Staring off into space, I said, "Sorry, I guess I'm just clutching at straws."

A caseworker for Missing and Exploited Children started on my brother's case the day after my mom reported him missing. She arranged for their posters to be put up all over the United States. Because of what Chief Randall had said about Curtis, they had to use the wording "Endangered Runaway."

My brother disappeared in 1990. As the family got caught up in this terrible trauma, I thought I would go insane. I hated the police because they wouldn't do anything about my brother, and Don was still walking around free. Every day it tore at my insides, knowing that he did something to Curtis, and we didn't have a clue where he was.

Three years dragged by without any resolution, and anger was just eating away at me. Anger had been a huge problem for me even before my brother vanished. I grew up in a dysfunctional family in Los Angeles. My dad was an abusive alcoholic. We eventually moved to Blue Lake in Northern California, where my mom had spent her childhood and still had family.

It was late in 1990 that I met Tim. We were both alcoholics and we both did drugs. Relationships like these are never good.

One day, I was so overcome with the hopelessness of our lifestyle, I just came out with it.

"Tim, we need to quit."

"We've already tried that," he replied, taking a drag on a joint.

"We went to counseling and went to AA." I didn't tell him that I had already gone to an Indian shaman.

"Cindy, the only thing that's going to help us is to move. We need to get away from all of our tweaky friends and start fresh somewhere else."

We pulled out a map and picked out a town in the middle of Oregon. Madras. We moved, thinking it would straighten everything out. It was naïve and absurd. You can't run from your problems.

I was drinking more and more instead of less and less. One morning, I padded around in my bare feet, got the kids situated and then grabbed my stash of beer. Later in the morning, as I was lying in a stupor on the couch hugging my bottle of beer close to my chest, the phone rang.

"Whosis?"

"Cindy?"

"Hiya, Mama!"

"Cindy, listen to me. Frank was at a bar last night and he heard a guy talk about how he and Don killed Curtis!"

"You serious?" I tried to clear my head, tried to focus my eyes.

"Yes! The man doing the talking was Mark. Remember him?"

"Yes!" I swung my legs from the couch to the floor and stood up. I felt suddenly alert as my mind frantically raced to remember what I could about Mark. "He was a kid who hung out a lot with Don. Right after Curtis disappeared, he started driving around in a nice, classic old truck. Someone told me Don gave it to him."

"Well, anyway, Frank said he is willing to do whatever it takes to help us get them. Mark said they 'dusted' Curtis!"

My mom called the police department right away. They took a statement from Frank and started a new investigation.

At that time, I decided my relationship wasn't going to work. I tried a couple of times to tell Tim, but something always interfered.

One Friday afternoon, we had been drinking and we had a nasty fight. We were supposed to go to a friend's house to party. We slammed out of the house into a gorgeous day. The skies were pale blue and the air was fresh with the scent of newly mowed grass. The cherry trees and dogwoods were showing off their new spring blooms in the most beautiful shades of pink.

I climbed into the car, tugged on the seatbelt and snapped it into place. I sat there like a stone, not saying a word to Tim.

Tim peeled out of the driveway and onto the highway. I stared out the window, wondering how to begin because I had decided now was the time to tell him I was going to leave him.

We were picking up speed, and I nervously watched the speedometer climb. The car swerved suddenly, and my hand shot out to brace myself on the dashboard. "@#?#@ squirrel!" Tim cussed.

He straightened out the car and I stared ahead at the road as I said, "I'm leaving you."

"I was wondering when you were going to say something."

"Did you hear what I said?"

He exhaled deeply. "Yes. Would it make any difference if I tried to talk you out of it?"

"No."

He made a sudden U-turn and headed back to the house. I packed up the kids and left for California the next day.

The morning the kids and I left, I started drinking as soon as I got up. We took a Greyhound Bus to California, and I stashed a bottle in my shoulder bag. Throughout the trip I drank and when we got off the bus, I was ready to cause someone some serious trouble.

After dropping my kids off with my parents, I went down to Don's house. There was a two-by-four outside his front door. I grabbed it and went into his house. I didn't bother to knock.

He was sitting in front of the TV. Brandishing the two-by-four, I confronted him. The booze fortified me, and I was burning like a raging fire, determined to get answers.

"Don, I want to know where my brother is. I know you killed him. I want to know what you did with him."

"I didn't kill him, Cindy!" He started scrambling, trying to get out of the recliner and as far away from me as possible.

I tracked him, keeping him within my reach. "Yeah, you did! Are you going to say my brother was a liar when he told my mom you molested him?"

He stopped moving and gave me a pleading, desperate look. Raising his arms, his palms up in some kind of surrendering gesture, he said, "Okay, I did molest him! But I didn't kill him!"

When I heard those words come out of his mouth, a red cloud of fury overcame me, and I started beating him with the two-by-four with all my strength. I chased him around the house, wielding my weapon.

Don ran into his garage and locked the door behind him.

Furious that he would hide from me, I took several swings at the items sitting on the counter, sending their pieces scattering across the room and stormed out the front door.

A very nice little sports car was parked in his driveway. It gleamed in the sun and seemed to beckon me. There was a woodpile next to the car where I found an axe and a log. As I heaved them both through the back window of his car, my energy was fueled by my hatred.

Leaving all the destruction behind me, I went to the police station. I was disheveled and noticed I had torn a big hole in my new, bright red Wal-Mart t-shirt.

"This guy has just told me he is a child molester. What are you going to do about it? You need to get down there right now."

Forgiving My Brother's Murderer

I had met the new chief of police before. "Cindy, what do you want me to do?"

"Do? There's a missing boy here and I want you to do your job and do whatever you can to find him! That's what I want you to do!" I cussed him out something awful.

He offered me nothing so I left, believing I would be going to jail that night because of all the destruction I caused at Don's place and, also, for the way I had talked to him.

Nothing happened. Absolutely nothing. Immediately, I thought, *If Don didn't kill my brother, I would be in jail right now. So the only reason I haven't been put in jail for destroying his property is because he did it and he doesn't want to press charges. The last thing he wants is any kind of involvement with the police.*

Meanwhile, the police had taken a statement from Frank, our friend who had overheard Mark admitting in the bar that he and Don had killed Curtis. They opened up a case on Curtis, but didn't make it a homicide.

My family became embroiled in a real fight. Or rather, it became my fight because my mom just buried herself in grief. She withdrew from the world. She had lost so much weight she was now down to less than 100 pounds. We fought on behalf of my brother all the way from City Hall to the Grand Jury. My dad was still drinking heavily. He and I had a tough time because he didn't understand why I was fighting the system. On my side, I was furious and didn't understand why he wasn't helping me take care of it. He had become apathetic.

I formed a peaceful march around the police station. Our small town of about 1,200 people knew a kid was missing. They knew he had been molested and probably killed, and no one was doing anything about it. It was in all the newspapers. After this march, the Grand Jury came, listened to the case, and it was then handed over to the FBI. They opened it up as a homicide case. That's when the search for my brother really began.

The search was a time of hope mixed with horror. Whenever bones or a body were discovered, we were called. Rumors were flying. The media was on our doorstep and called us on the phone all the time. We were not prepared for that gross intrusion into our lives.

That whole summer just dragged on with nothing really happening. Tim came from Madras to see me and saw I wasn't doing well at all.

"Cindy, this meth you're into is going to do you in. I love you. Our family needs to be together again. Come back to Oregon with me."

"Tim, I don't know if I should leave my mom. She can't handle this stuff."

"You got the ball rolling. Things are in the hands of the FBI, and the case will go forward according to their investigations. There's really nothing more you can do here. I need you now!"

He helped me pack my stuff, we piled the kids into the car and drove back to Oregon. As soon as we arrived, I started drinking very heavily. For two weeks, I just sat around drinking.

"'S'wayitgoes." In my alcoholic haze, I had knocked over my bottle of beer, and I just sat there watching the amber-colored liquid spread all over the coffee table. It saturated a magazine, then started dribbling from the edge of the table onto the carpet.

"Never shoulda left my mom. 'S'my 'sponsibility."

When I went to bed that night, I lay curled up into a

tight ball.

God, what am I doing? What's going on with my life?
All my life, my experience with God was along the lines of He's "up there" somewhere. If I bought a lotto ticket, I would pray, "God, please let me win!"

As I lay in my bed, lost and confused, the story of my life began to play itself through my mind like a movie.

When I was little, instead of playing "house," we played "drunk." I started drinking when I was 12. At age 14, I got pregnant for the first time. The father was 22, and I broke up with him before I realized I was pregnant. Still in high school, I made a wonderful new friend, Jeff. He and I talked a lot. I could confide in him. We played pool together. He wasn't into partying, and I didn't know very many people like that. Jeff accepted me with my pregnancy. We began to fall in love. He fathered my second child, and I was 16 when I had the baby. After my second child was born, I got really bad with my drinking. Jeff, the two kids and I lived down the road from my mom. The whole summer we lived together was a blackout to me, and I wasn't even aware when he left me. I didn't care and that's when I met Tim.

My house had been the party house for the town. One night, a bunch of us were partying, and I was drinking Jack Daniels and Black Velvet straight from the bottles. I had a "thing" going with the Jack Daniels bottles. There was a tower in my living room that I had built by stacking empty bottles of Jack Daniels, and I was proud of it. As the party went on around me, I was suddenly overcome with despair. Thinking to myself that there was no way out, I began to slowly, methodically break those bottles, one at a time. Then I took a broken bottle with a jagged neck and cut one of my wrists. Blood started spurting all over the place. It took me a moment to realize what I had just done as a stream quickly poured from my fingers. I put my other hand over my wrist and tried to stop the bleeding, but it was just uncontrollably shooting out.

As I ran out of the house screaming, a couple of my friends followed me and tried to help. I ran from them and tried to hide. "No! No!" I was in shock.

There was a creek that ran under a building, and I ran and hid in the dry creek bed. I just wanted to lie down and die. I could hear the search going on for me. The paramedics found me and rushed me to the hospital. It took 32 stitches to close up my wound. I was 16 years old.

One of the worst moments in my life was when I woke up in that hospital and everything in the room, including the windows, was covered with padding. There was a tiny window in the door with bars on it. I was so drugged up with whatever they gave me that I felt like I weighed a million pounds. It took everything I had just to get up. The night before was just a big fog to me. My wrist was all bandaged, and as I lowered my gaze to stare at it, I tried to remember what happened.

While these horrible tapes of my life were running through my mind, I finally fell asleep.

When I woke up the next morning, it was a Monday, and I went through the motions of feeding the kids breakfast and making my drinking plan for the day. A knock at the front door really irritated me. I was hung over and crabby and when I yanked the front door open, a young man was standing there. He was about 16, had a pimply face and he stuttered. He reached his hands out to me. "C-c-can I p-p-pray for you?"

"Who are you, and why are you at my door?" His

hands were still reaching out to me. Surprisingly, I decided to put the tips of my fingers into his palms because I didn't want to touch him, and I didn't want him to touch me. I believed if I did this we would get it over with quickly. I had to fight the desire to slam the door in his face.

He began to pray. His words didn't make any sense to me, so I just watched him. His eyes were tightly closed and he was trying so hard. He was stuttering out the words and it was taking forever. I remember thinking, *Come on! Let's get this over with!*

"In the name of Jesus Christ, I rebuke the devil. Come out of this house! Holy Spirit of God, You are welcome in this place."

That got my attention. I didn't know what any of it meant, but I'll never forget hearing those words. And then I closed my eyes.

"God, if You are real and You want me, You will have to take me off drugs and alcohol."

Instantly, a change came over me! Something beautiful and loving started to bathe me from the tips of my toes to the top of my head. A feeling of peace consumed me, and I felt rather than heard the words, *It's going to be okay.*

There was this feeling inside me that God had just answered me.

I am real.

When I opened my eyes, the boy, still fidgety and nervous, spun around on his heel and left quickly.

Earlier, I had packed all my stuff because I knew it wasn't going to work out with Tim. I had been feeling so awful that day from drinking all night, plus emotional distress, but I felt better all of a sudden. Everything *is* going to be okay!

Tim was working the swing shift. While waiting for him, I unpacked my things and cleaned the house. My spirits were higher than they had been for years. I heard Tim wiping his feet on the mat on the front porch. As soon as the door opened, I said, "We need to go to church or it's never going to work with us."

"Okay." That's all he said. Just like that! We stopped drinking and using drugs.

For three days after the boy's visit, I was totally overcome by the fact that God loved me. That He was real. His love melted my heart, and I found I was capable of loving others in a way I would have never believed had anyone tried to tell me. On the third day of this "love high," it hit me.

This is God we're talking about here. He knows everything! Astonishment, humiliation and utter disgrace forced me down to my living room floor where I stretched myself out, nose to the carpet. The things I had done started going through my mind. Many of those things only He and I knew about. Horrible things I had done while drinking and taking drugs.

"Oh, God! I am so sorry!" The words came out of my mouth in an agony of repentance and anguish as I pounded on the floor with my fists.

"Wait a minute," I said to myself. "He forgave me three days ago when I asked Him to be real for me. Just because I can remember all those horrible things doesn't lessen His love for me." That started the most amazing and blessed experience of receiving His forgiveness. *God, who knows and sees everything, loves me and has forgiven me!* At that point, no one had to tell me what it was like to be a Christian.

Forgiving My Brother's Murderer

When Sunday came, Tim and I had no idea where to go to church. There was a lady I had known before I left Tim for five months to be in California. She was someone from work who had invited me to church.

"Hey, that girl I used to work with invited me to go to church. Let's go to that one."

We pulled up to the church and heard music coming out. "Oh, we're late! We can't go in!" We didn't know it was okay to arrive late, so we left there and went to another church we had passed on the way, checked out the starting time and saw that it was going to start in 30 minutes. We went to that service. None of it made any sense to us, but it felt nice and the people looked so happy.

The next Sunday we made it to the other church on time. They sang "Amazing Grace," and the pastor said if anyone wanted to give their life to God to please come forward to say the sinner's prayer. Tim and I went up and prayed together. It was quite a feeling making a commitment to God in public, and the fact that we did it together was huge.

The pastor of the church and I had a talk one day, and I told him about my missing brother and the hatred I had in my heart for Don. It was now three years after my brother's disappearance

"You need to forgive that man, Cindy."

"How can I do that? How can I forgive a child molester and murderer?"

"If you are in Christ and He is in you, you have to forgive that man just as you have been forgiven by Him."

We attended services there for a few months and then Tim's supervisor invited us to try his church.

On a night in the middle of the week, Tim and I had a spat. In the past, when that happened I would leave and go get drunk. This time I wheeled our motorcycle out of the garage, hopped on and decided to take a ride and see if I could find Tim's supervisor's church. When I found it, I felt a little conspicuous pulling up on the motorcycle, and I couldn't help wondering what people there would think of me.

Any self-conscious thought I might have entertained left me the minute I stepped inside the church. God's love poured out of every nook and cranny of that church. Beautiful music reached out and pulled me into the sanctuary. Someone was playing drums and another person was playing the guitar. Words to the songs were being shown on a screen, and the sound of the music and singing, the genuine praise and worship, swept over me and touched a place inside me that had never been touched before. Tears ran down my cheeks. The words to the songs penetrated my soul and pierced my heart. The music told me, *This is it. This is our church.* I knew, without a doubt, Tim would feel the same way. Our new church was now Living Hope Christian Center. After attending for a short time, Tim and I married.

From 1990 to 1993, the case for my brother was an emotional roller coaster. Whenever bones were found we would get a call. Once, some bones were uncovered in a mound of dirt and gravel. They said it looked like a spine. Our family was called to the site and by the time we arrived, half the town had showed up. They circled around like vultures and watched as the FBI dusted with their brushes. When they uncovered the whole find, they had to call the coroner because they couldn't tell what kind of bones they were looking at.

Forgiving My Brother's Murderer

My heart was racing. *Oh my God, could this be him?* All of us were on edge and grieving, but hopeful. When we received the call telling us they were animal bones, we found ourselves down in the depths of despair once again.

We went through this repeatedly, and every time it happened, we just knew that "this time" they had finally found Curtis. We would have closure, we would be able to bury him and have a memorial for him.

In 1996, a man by the name of Mike Fox was arrested and convicted of murdering an 11-year-old boy. That name got my attention. Back in 1993, when I had done my own investigating, Mike Fox's name came up and I passed it on to the FBI. He had been a good friend of Don's and he was related to Mark, the young man Don had given the truck to, and who later did the bragging in the bar. Also, Mike Fox had Mark move in with him after my brother disappeared, so he was in the circle of people directly related to my brother's death.

When Mike Fox was arrested, they searched his home and found hundreds and hundreds of child pornography pictures. As a result of the FBI's investigations, they discovered he had been chloroforming young boys and then taking pictures of them. We had a gut feeling that my brother was part of all that.

The investigation was sealed until they could make sure that every boy was accounted for. Then the newspaper printed an article saying all the boys had been identified. But we still had this gut feeling.

Mike Fox later told the police that my brother was in those pictures they had found in his house, so my mother and I had to go look at them. These children were so defiled. There was one picture of a young boy who was about the same age as my son. The picture of him was from the waist up. His hands were tied and he was hanging from a hook in the ceiling. He was unconscious. I just stared and stared at those chubby, little boy cheeks. I had nightmares after that. The authorities had made it very public that all these boys had been accounted for, but there were four pictures that were not accounted for. We had to look for something, anything that would identify Curtis. Mike Fox insisted that Curtis was in these photos. There were some pictures that could have been him, but we couldn't say so with 100 percent certainty.

While he was in prison on death row, Mike Fox wrote a letter revealing his feelings about killing Curtis and another boy, Danny Williams. We were stunned when we heard about it.

He talked about the night my brother died. He said he was at Don's house, and Don chloroformed my brother and then did things to him. Mike said when Curtis woke up, he was throwing up, grabbed his things and ran out the door. Then he said Curtis came back with a gun and they all wrestled trying to get control of it. Mike said he was trying to stop Curtis from shooting Don and that he accidentally pulled the trigger and shot Curtis in the heart. After that, he helped Don put Curtis in the bathtub, and then he left. During this whole thing, Mike said Mark was present and watching the entire time. As part of his letter, Mike drew a diagram of where the shooting occurred in Don's house.

When the FBI got that letter with Mike's confession, they talked to him and then they began an investigation of both Mike and Don. When they talked to Don, he told them Mike had never even been in his house, but he did acknowledge that they were friends.

During this period of time, I was living in Oregon. My mother had recently become a Christian, and I was thrilled that she now had the peace and love of God in her heart. One morning, I gave her a call. I wanted to share something about the Lord with her. Her phone rang and rang, but she didn't answer.

As Mom walked out her front door she heard the phone ringing. She disregarded it as she scuffed along the road in her thong sandals, a fine film of dust settling on her exposed feet. The morning was hot and it seemed to intensify the sweet fragrance of honeysuckle growing nearby. She loved honeysuckle, and it saddened her to think she might always associate it with times of grief and sorrow.

When she reached Don's house, she flung open the gate to the yard, walked up to the front porch and knocked on the door.

Don answered her knock and when he opened the door, he stepped back as if he had been struck. "Nancy!"

"May I come in please?"

"Uh... sure. Come in." He stepped aside so she could enter the house. He stood there nervously rubbing one forearm with his hand. His face was pinched and pale looking.

Mom remained standing. She locked her gaze onto his and said, "Don, just tell me where my boy is so I can bury him properly and that will be the end of it. It will just be over."

This was the first time she had talked to him since all this happened. She was offering him an "out" if he would tell her where the remains were. Because she had found the Lord, it wasn't about justice or getting Don anymore. It was about taking care of her son's remains and letting God control the rest. She just wanted her boy.

"I didn't kill him, Nancy!" He looked like a deer suddenly caught in the headlights of a car as he watched her get down on her knees, hands clasped together as if in prayer. She started to cry.

"I'm begging you to just tell me where my son is!"

"Nancy, don't!" Sweat was forming in his armpits.

"I need to bury my son, Don! Please!"

"Okay." Waves of nausea undulated in his gut as he gave up. There was no turning back now.

After that one word answer, neither of them spoke. They went out to his car. He helped her into it and started driving. The scenery alongside the road was breathtaking. The redwood groves grew close to the roadside. There was a rich understory of fir, huckleberry and evergreen bushes, sword fern and an abundance of greenery. A tear slid out of the corner of each of Mom's eyes. How could such evil, yes, death itself, be found in a beautiful place like this?

Soon, Don was pulling off to the side of the road. When he parked, he stood quietly beside the car as Mom slammed the door on her side behind her. She fell into step with him as he made his way into the forest area. They hadn't gone far when he stopped next to a tree stump in a small clearing. "I buried Curtis there."

Mom approached the stump with a feeling of reverence and an agony of grief. She fell to her knees, and leaning on the tree stump with both arms laid out in front her, she rested her head on them and cried softly. "Curtis? Oh, my baby! Are you really there?"

Forgiving My Brother's Murderer

Don couldn't stand to watch. Tears were streaming down his face, and he backed off several paces and turned his back. He didn't want to violate the grief of this mother who had been his friend. He felt like he was soiling something holy and sanctified just with his presence. He didn't hear her approach from behind, but felt a soft touch on his arm. Neither of them spoke. They walked in silence back to the car.

Driving her home, when Don felt he could speak again, he said, "Nancy, would you please wait until midnight before you call the cops?"

Instead of answering, her voice soft but clear, she said, "Don, do I sense a suicide spirit about you?"

He was reluctant, but finally said, "Yeah, you do."

"You don't want to do that, Don. You are only thinking about yourself when you do that. Families suffer terribly once someone commits suicide." She was trying to change his mind.

My mom called me as soon as Don dropped her off back at her house.

"Are you really going to wait until midnight to call the police?"

"What should I do, Cindy?"

"You need to call now!"

While listening to my mom on the phone, I didn't want to discourage her spiritually because she was doing so well, but I kept thinking, *He deserves to die! Let him kill himself!*

That hatred was beginning to seep back into my heart again, and I knew I was going to have to get rid of it. After I hung up, I got on my knees in front of my couch.

"God, I am not going to move until You put Your forgiveness in me because I cannot let myself go back to the hateful person I was."

For hours I sat there praying. "God, fill my heart with Your forgiveness, the forgiveness I received from You. Give me that kind of forgiveness for Don. I don't have it, God. I can't forgive someone who molested and murdered my brother." I stayed there until He gave it to me. Then I got up and called my mother back.

"I'll be there tomorrow."

It was okay with my husband, so I left the next morning. My mom had called the police after we talked on the phone, and they put crime scene tape around the area where Don said he buried my brother. In the meantime, Don had disappeared and his picture was being shown on TV.

I went to his house, talked with his wife and shared the Lord with her. She told me Don had said he was going to commit suicide, and we talked about that for a while. I talked to her about the Lord and she was very receptive.

My family went up to the area where Don had taken my mom. It was an area we had searched ourselves, and so had Chief Randall in 1990. At least there was a report in the file that said he searched there. That report mentioned the discovery of some blood that went across the road and into this particular area. The chief said he checked on it, and that someone's dog died and they buried it there.

We all took shovels and dug and dug, but didn't find anything. Some neighbors came along, also. We spent the entire day digging, but didn't find a thing.

The police were looking for Don and hadn't started digging on their own yet. The thought occurred to me that Don might have been lying to us and had fled to avoid being arrested. I went down to his house to question his wife again, and on the way, I couldn't help thinking, *Where is this guy who said he buried my brother? There's nothing there!*

As we talked quietly, Don walked through the door. Tears were running down his face as he told us he had gone to the top of the mountain to kill himself.

"I couldn't do it!" He flung himself against the wall and pounded on it with his fists. "I tried, but I just couldn't do it!"

Watching him, I knew I should have been feeling compassion, but all I could do was say, "Okay, but you said you buried my brother in a spot you showed to my mom. We dug all day and he's not there. Take me! Show me!"

My mom, Don and I went back up there and he pointed out the same stump. It wasn't very far off the road.

"I know it's right here!" He was looking frantically, turning in confused circles, as he trembled violently.

As I watched Don, I just had this incredible thought. *How is it possible that I am here in this forest with this man? He's a murderer and we are looking for my brother!* It was surreal.

We were standing under a canopy of redwood trees. Shafts of sunlight were filtering through them, and as I looked, there seemed to be an inner light emanating from them. Within seconds, the light concentrated right on the area where we were standing. There had been a gentle swishing noise as the wind blew gently through the trees, but now the breeze had died into total stillness. I felt like I was in a heavenly cathedral. Then I became aware of His presence, the radiance of His glory; I was consumed with His love.

Turning to look at Don again, my heart spoke to me. *This man needs God's forgiveness. If Jesus was to come back tonight, and Don doesn't know the Lord, he'll go to hell. Knowing the Lord is more important than finding my brother. There's nothing we can do for Curtis now, but there is something we can do for this man.*

"Don, we need to stop what we are doing right now. I want to ask you, if you are willing, to give your heart to the Lord."

My mother started to pray for him.

Wiping his eyes, he gave me a startled, unbelieving look. "How could God want me after what I have done?"

"Let me tell you about some people in the Bible that God actually loved and used, and because of what they have shared, we can be saved." I told him about David and Paul. "I don't know how many people you have killed, Don, but these people killed many."

He just stood there, shaking, tears pouring out of his eyes.

"Don, do you want to give God a chance and give Him your life?"

"Yes!" he cried out in a hoarse voice.

We said the sinner's prayer with him and then something amazing happened. I began to feel a sincere, genuine love for this man. I couldn't explain it. This consuming love I was feeling wasn't a choice I made. It was just happening. I cared about his soul.

It was astonishing to realize that for years we had fought the police to get this man. Now we were standing in a marked-off crime scene with him, and we had led him to the Lord. We cared about him.

Forgiving My Brother's Murderer

We got him back into the car, and at that very moment, a police officer showed up. They had been searching for Don all day. My mom and I went to talk to the officer. "He's over there in the car. He showed us the exact spot where he buried my brother. We just prayed for him and he needs to regroup."

It seemed incredible that the officer would let us drive off with Don, but he didn't attempt to remove him from the car. We didn't know it at the time, but the FBI had to be notified because they were in charge of the case.

The next day, there were tons of people heading to the forest area where Don said he buried Curtis. There was a long line of vehicles that were going to be involved in the search — the FBI, the sheriff, the forensic team and search and rescue.

Finally, after all these years, there was a small army that would find my brother, and he could be laid to rest.

We were told later that after Curtis had been murdered, Don took out the wall that would have been behind my brother at the time of the shooting. Because of that, the forensics team had cut a piece out of the floor where human blood had been found. They took it with them.

All these people combed the area for his remains. They looked for hours. There was nothing.

Unbelievably, the piece of floor got lost somehow. My mom went to the DA's office and demanded that they find it. Not only that, but the files in the DA's office were gone. All the parts and pieces of my brother's case were missing. To this day, nothing has happened. Don has never seen a judge and has done no time in jail. We still haven't found Curtis and there is no closure.

My mom hasn't seen Don, and we don't know if he still owns the house down the road. She has heard that he's still around, but she hasn't run into him.

When my husband and I became Christians, I started working with women for about 10 years to help them with their pain, and then I shifted my focus to working on the reservation with Native American youth. I am able to communicate to them that they are valuable and they have worth. If I can keep even one kid from going down the wrong road, I will be happy. I minister to the Native American people that already have burdens because of their race. I can almost see Curtis in all of them. I can see his face today. *Help me. Please, help me.* I couldn't see that before. I wasn't there for him. I didn't help him that night. I can't do anything for him now, but I can do something for the ones that are still out there.

I can share the freedom that forgiveness brings. I can remind them that life is full of unfair and painful times that make us bitter or better. The choice is ours. My family has now grown to six children. If you ask my older children what I have taught them as words to live by, they would tell you, "Love all people, and forgive all wrongs... quickly." With God, all things are possible.

Drive By

John David Urrutia-Carrasco's story
as told by Richard Drebert

Ephesians 6:12: "For we wrestle not against flesh and blood, but against principalities, against powers, against the rulers of the darkness of this world, against spiritual wickedness..."

El Diablo In My Barrio

The devil, El Diablo, shows himself differently to people in the barrio (neighborhood) where I grew up. He wears baggy pants and a blue bandana. His black hair may be slicked back or his head prison-shaved, and he struts to his own corrupting rap. He commands respect on the streets, and families fear him. Gold chains dangle from his neck, maybe even a crucifix. Barbed wire tattoos his biceps. Graffiti of snakes, women and gang emblems tattoo his bare shoulders. A sneer is sculpted in his face, hard, like bronze, yet his eyes are seductive.

Children who live in my barrio on Vaughn Street, Pacoima, run behind him, hoping The Gangster notices them. He holds out his hands to hijos (sons) and hijas (daughters), and when they reach out to him, mothers weep. The Gangster closes the door of his house with their ninos (little ones) inside, and parents know that their children will live and die for The Gangster with other "homies" (trusted comrades) in his house. Their hijos and hijas believe they belong to him forever, and they fear what will happen to them if they leave his "protection."

Many of my loved ones at home in Pacoima, San Fernando, California, have accepted the protection of The Gangster: aunts, uncles and my two dear brothers. As a boy, I wanted to be like The Gangster, too. No one

Drive By

could *stomp* him. No one dared disrespect him. But as I watched him, a Voice in my soul said, "Miho, you are not created for this. You are mine." And I listened to The Voice. When I was 14 years old, far away from gang life, I found out that this Voice was Jesus — mi Salvador (my Savior).

Angelica's Familia

Five girls slunk from the shadows to circle Angelica Urrutia and two friends.

"You Chicas lost?" they taunted, and Angelica knew that she could die here, right now. Broken glass from a street lamp crunched beneath her tennis shoes, and she stared hard at the hands of the five girls. In the evening half-light, she detected no knives, and it would be hard to hide guns in their tight clothing, so she decided to risk it. Her sisters began hurling Chicano curses, and Angelica slammed her knuckles into the nose of the tallest rival gang-banger, and began to kick.

"Angelica. What...?"

My mama slumped in the doorway of the house, her tank top stretched and torn. Red claw marks streaked her bare arms and neck, and blood matted her black hair. She swiped at tear-glazed eyes, glad that none of her homies could see. Sternly, my grandmother led Mama to their kitchen, and ran warm water. She dabbed at her daughter's wounds and blood turned the white towel crimson. Grandmother shook her head reproachfully. It did no good to scold Angelica again. At 13 years old, my mama belonged to a street gang called The Hart Street Locas.

Grandmother glimpsed a reflection of herself in her

child's face, the stubborn set of her jaw and a look of daggers in her expression. Each were surviving the best way they knew how in the barrio. Grandmother had arrived with her family in Pacoima, San Fernando Valley, from Mexico, when she was in her 30s, and Mama was 6 years old. As a Roman Catholic, she had instilled in Angelica that God was real, but prayer beads and catechism did little to fill the hunger in her daughter's heart. Angelica sought protection on the streets, and wanted to *belong*. It was the same yearning that Grandmother felt; the same need that most other Chicanos in the barrio know.

To my grandmother's sorrow, her daughter found kinship with The Hart Street Locas. Her homies would watch her back, and they would defend her. Angelica shared tradition with her homies, and confided common fears and hurts. Gangsters became Mama's familia, and she became pregnant when she was just 14.

At the time, Grandmother couldn't have known that Mi Salvador was calling to Mama's heart, just as He had been calling to her own. Angelica began praying to God, pleading for His help, and after her beautiful baby boy was born, gang life lost its allure. In a few years, Mama met a carpenter named Gabriel, a Christian man, my father. Mama and my grandmother accepted the true Protector, Jesus Christ, and my father and mother started a *real* familia.

The Gangster House

The way Mama raised us five boys, we never would have believed that she lived the life of a street gangster.

Drive By

Not tiny, straight-laced Angelica Urrutia-Carrasco who was quiet, strong-willed and a woman of prayer. And I can't imagine living with 17 brothers and sisters, like my father did when he was a boy. He was one of the oldest in a Christian family, born in Chihuahua Juarez, Mexico. He seldom missed a day of work, starting at 5 years old, laboring in the fields. Papa received his green card in the States at about 18, and his talents as a builder landed him a career as a contractor in the San Fernando Valley. Mama stayed home to raise their sons.

"Out of bed, boys!"

Papa's work ethic blended with his spiritual life, so my four brothers and I became regular churchgoers, too, whenever he was home. Papa helped build the Living Word of Zion Church, and it stood as a white beacon of hope in our barrio.

My family lived in an old district of the San Fernando Valley that the Chamber of Commerce hoped to rehabilitate, or rip out of the phone book altogether. Known as Pacoima, it lay in the northeast portion of San Fernando, dominated by Latinos and their cultures, and infamous for headlines about drug busts and gang murders. Not far from our church, my grandmother rented a home on Vaughn Street, a rundown suburb that made some of "the projects" seem pristine.

Vaughn Street became our barrio, a place where I spent half my life, and where my family has always called home. Whenever a friend or relative needed help, they moved to Grandmother's to heal up, body and soul. Her old, beige-colored, four-bedroom house became a haven for my mama when Papa was away working, and we often stayed with Grandmother when finances were tight.

A searing California summer sun baked Grandmother's half-naked, barefoot grandchildren as dark as fresh bread from her oven. We tore up and down Vaughn Street every day, late into the stifling, humid nights, crazy with fun, playing baseball, street hockey, tag and soccer with our homies. In the fall, my mother enrolled us in Pacoima schools, notorious for gang violence and monstrous student-to-teacher ratios.

I loved my life on Vaughn Street. Wide-eyed and surrounded by family, I believed I had it all. But El Diablo saw promise in my Vaughn Street barrio, too. I don't remember when the ill-famed Pacoima Vaughn Street Gang staked its headquarters next door to my grandmother, but the boys and girls of our barrio were enthralled. The hoodlums who worked in the Gang House drove fine low-riders, and played loud rap, and many of us hoped that someday we too might be *their* homies.

How Tough Are You?

The oldest Chicano gangs boast of a lawless heritage, harking back to when Mexican banditos dodged the noose in California in the late 1800s. Rivalries between gangs are legendary in San Fernando, and bloody battles, called turf wars, are still fought over crack houses, party spots, drug corners or graffiti. Often, newspaper stories give the false impression that street gangs exist as isolated groups, tending toward chaos. But in cities like San Fernando, gangs are structured like cells in a frantic beehive, loosely tied to richer, more powerful Mexican gangs in greater Los Angeles that may demand tribute for their protection.

The richest recruiting ground for street gangs is prison, where a "wannabe" gangster can climb to "hardcore" before hitting the streets after his parole. Dirty -ink graffiti embroidered upon skin is a badge of honor when a gang-banger returns to their barrio after doing hard time. On the streets, hardcore veteranos (veterans) train and nurture new gangsters in trash talk, street fighting, theft, drug trafficking, and in some cases, murder. "Fight or Die" is their creed meaning if your homies are "in" for a fight, you better fight, too. If someone threatens to move in on your territory, it's Fight or Die. Veteranos drill you on the three R's of gang life: Reputation, Respect and Retaliation.

Fear taunts a gang-banger every waking moment of his or her confused life.

"How tough are you?" Fear whispers long after your gang initiation, when five or more of your trusted homies "jumped" you into the club. They punched you to a pulp on this day of bloody initiation. You fought back to survive the test, adrenaline pumping and your fists flailing. You were a spectacle for leering veteranos and gang members. In the end, you dragged yourself from the alley, bleeding, but cheered for your machismo, if that is what the veteranos saw. If not, you were marked as weak and had to prove yourself another way.

Want out of your gang? Tell the priest to prepare a eulogy and help your family choose a coffin. It may be the only way a hardcore gang-banger can quit. Petty thugs with little respect, who live on the fringes of gang life, fair better than veteranos who "desert" their homies for a fresh start. Gang leaders suspect veteranos who desert because they "know where the bodies are buried." They have broken trust and become weak. A gang "deserter" may trade damning information to the authorities in exchange for police protection.

Drive-By Drill

"Looks like they got a new TV," my older brother said under his breath. Two brawny gangsters seemed to be nearly losing their baggy pants as they hefted a widescreen through the doorway of the Gang House. We envied their bulging muscles, revealed by skimpy, white tank tops, and we hoped to strut the neighborhood in expensive Nike tennis shoes like theirs someday. No one usually loitered outside the seedy, blue and white Gang House, but music bumped night and day and we wondered what it looked like inside.

"I wonder where they got it," I whispered.

"Don't ask, John David. Okay?"

I nodded. My older brother already knew the unspoken rule that all gangsters live by: *Don't ask questions.* I knew he was watching my back. He always did.

Boys and girls were gathering to play out in the street, and we could already fry an egg on the sidewalk though it was still morning. We ignored the sweat streaming down our sides as we chose up teams for a game of baseball. Some of us were pretty good, and in the back of our minds, we wondered if one or two of us might attain notoriety outside the barrio. Bobby Chacon had done it, and our grandfathers would never let us forget him. He was a world featherweight champion boxer from Pacoima.

Then there was Ritchie Valens, the famous rock and

Drive By

roll singer from Pacoima, who died in a plane crash when he was just 17 years old. Our swooning grandmothers would never let us forget *him*. (Later, our hometown would be proud of Pacoima's George Lopez, comedian and TV star.)

I was about to take the batter's box, when a scream creased the air.

"Drive-by!"

Like ants in a rainstorm, we scattered into houses, under porches and behind parked cars. We peeked out from our hiding places, aiming make-believe Uzis and shotguns at a green Chevy Malibu as it uttered a deafening tailpipe burst and trundled by. Behind the wheel, an old man in a baseball cap snarled at us as we re-gathered on the street, laughing and jibing one another about our "drive-by." We loved the drill, and no matter what we were playing, if a car dropped its speed near us, our game required us to warn the others and hide.

Even in our play, we were being schooled in surviving the cruel streets without our realizing it. A gang-banger father of one of my playmates had taught the game to his son. I thought it was a great addition to our daily games, until a real drive-by changed my life.

Blood On Our Block

I wish that we had been playing outside to warn my homie that day. I looked up to my older friend, who claimed the barrio streets and dirt yards as his private bicycle racetrack. He was 14 years old when rivals of the Pacoima Vaughn Street Gang gunned him down near Grandmother's house. Mama heard the gunshots first.

She snatched us up from rooms all over the house, like garments off a clothesline, and flung us into a back bedroom. Sharp reports from a semiautomatic kept us on the floor as bullets thwacked the front siding of the house. Seconds later, a fresh and more sustained volley erupted from the Gang House next door. A car engine roared triumphantly, then faded away to leave our barrio silent and breathless. None of us moved until my older brother stood up to go outside.

"DOWN!" Mama said in a loud whisper, still hugging my two toddler brothers to her chest. As familiar, muffled voices drifted in from outdoors, Grandmother rose slowly from her knees.

"I'll go see," she said.

Distant sirens warned that the police knew about the exchange of gunfire, and Pacoima gang members congregated briefly in front of the Gang House to get their stories straight if they were questioned. A few of them, with bulges in their shirts, jumped into cars and sped away.

"You stay inside. Watch your brothers, you hear?" Mama ordered. We three older boys nodded as we watched her leave the room. Immediately, we herded our younger siblings into the living room and crept up behind Mama, who seemed devastated by the scene outside. We peeked past her out the open door.

The police had arrived quickly, and neighbors peeked timidly from behind curtained windows along the street. The scene somehow reminded me of a horror movie where everyone waited for a monster to appear, and I moved to our window to see what everyone was staring at. On the sidewalk between Grandmother's home and the Gang House, a bloodstained sheet draped someone. I knew the tennis shoes and the bicycle lying beside him.

No one was arrested from the Gang House. The next day, we played all around the dark spot on the ground where my friend had bled to death. My barrio accepted that someone would die in a drive-by from time to time, and as the days passed, we forgot about the murder, but not the gang-bangers next door. They felt that their home turf had been violated. Inside their house they paced, posted extra guards and schemed revenge.

The murder of my friend had a chilling effect upon me as I realized that the powerful Vaughn Street Pacoima Gang couldn't protect my barrio or my family. This had been my first *real* drive-by, and I knew that it wouldn't be my last if I embraced the lifestyle of a gangster. Uncertainty, fear and grief awaited me in just a few years, and in my young heart, I began to articulate a vow: *I would never join a gang, even if my Chicano brothers and sisters accused me of being disloyal.* I cherished my Chicano heritage, and I had been immersed in a sense of care and community that I would always treasure, but it wasn't enough.

Next door at the Gang House, the gang-bangers stoked up the fires of revenge. Some were gangster "dads" of my homies that I played ball with. I didn't understand that under the sneers and swaggers, they were afraid. They feared going to prison. They lived with the fear of looking weak or breaking a gang code. They worried over losing a child in a drive-by or dying in a fight. Fear had kept most of my Mexican family ensnared in gang life for generations, but how could we escape this *destino* (destiny)?

You are not created for this, Jesus said to my heart,

and childlike, I waited for God to do the impossible.

Green Light

Sometimes I think that El Diablo proclaimed a spiritual "green light" upon my mama and papa, like the powerful gang leaders often did in the San Fernando Valley. Among the hundreds of gangs, if a renegade gangster trespassed on another gang's turf without clearing it with their leadership, they had to pay for their indiscretion. The accusing gang might petition all the gangs in a district to declare a green light on the offenders. This meant that the offenders became fair game to every gang-banger who wanted to get their hands dirty. Chase them down, kill them or maim them on the streets, but make the culprits pay for breaking the gangsters' twisted code.

Both my mama and papa were God-fearing Christians, churchgoers and praying people. Their examples as a married couple in the barrio infuriated The Gangster, and he set out to take back his turf. He used life's circumstances to blind my mother and father to their powerful effect for Christ among Chicano families, and set out to break them apart.

How would my life be different if my father had stayed with Mama and his five sons? I don't know. To this day, I don't understand the reasons why my parents divorced. Was it my fault? Should I have been a more obedient son to make my father stay? For years, questions like these plagued me after he moved away. All I know is that when my father came home after working, my parents stopped talking together, except to quarrel.

Drive By

When Papa moved away, The Gangster saw his chance with two of my brothers. He strutted past Grandmother's house, beckoning them to take his hand, and my mama watched his antics. She knew that, in the end, he would murder all her boys if he could. The longer we stayed with Grandmother, next to the Gang House, the closer my brothers gravitated to their new "father figures," veterano gang-bangers, tough-talking and protective. Grandmother saw it happening, too.

New Start, Old Threats

My little barrio homies danced around my father's pickup, tripping up the men stuffing the last mattress into the truck bed. I was in third grade when Mama risked everything to move us to Madras, Oregon. She had little money, and our only connection to the town was a childhood friend of my grandmother. Mama had visited Madras once as a girl, and she remembered the rich, green fields of hay, corn and potatoes. And the mountains! Everywhere, there was clean air that you could almost taste and grand peaks that stood as sentries on the horizon.

My two youngest brothers were barely daycare age. I was 9 and my two other brothers were 8 and 13 years old. Mama could imagine her sons standing on those peaks and experiencing God's beauty for the first time, away from the squalor of Pacoima. At new schools, they could seize the opportunity to learn and not fight. They could *graduate,* go to the community college and get a good job and … So many prayers to pray for her ninos! Madras was small, but she hoped to find work in the fields or at a motel in Bend, a metropolis nearby.

It seemed as if the whole barrio had come outside to see us off. Grandmother stood with arms folded against her blue, flowered apron, and I rolled down the pickup window. She brushed away a strand of dark hair that had escaped bobby pins as she came close.

"You know I'm here if you need me."

"We know, Gramma," my older brother said. "We'll be okay. No crying now."

Papa started the engine.

An uncle had driven Mama and my two younger brothers to Madras days before. Mama's excited words on the phone had tumbled like potatoes from a sack about how wonderful the rivers were and how she had "found a place to rent, and maybe a church, and maybe a job and..."

Even though divorced, my parents remained friends. Papa worried over his sons' futures, too, agreeing with Mama that moving to Madras might be the best chance their boys had of avoiding gang life. He also knew that when Angelica believed that God was the wind beneath her wings, nothing could change her course. Papa agreed to help us move wherever Mama landed.

"You boys be good! You hear me? No fighting." We grinned at Grandmother as Papa pulled away. At the Gang House, three men slouched against a parked low-rider, and they nodded at my two brothers, who flashed them gang signs. Papa scowled.

Tops Trailer Court in Madras, Oregon, was our new barrio, minus our homies tearing around on bikes and playing baseball on the hot pavement. Also absent from our neighborhood was Grandmother's house to hide in when things got tough. To us, the block seemed deserted, like everyone expected a drive-by any minute. A familiar unease settled on us as we carried our belongings into one of the tiny trailer bedrooms, and Mama read the worry in our three faces.

"This is just until we can afford to rent a bigger place. I have an interview for a job at Bright Wood next week. This is a brand new life for us, mijos. We must leave our old lives behind us."

She didn't need to spell it out. We knew what she meant by "old lives." All three of us had begun to experiment with marijuana, and fighting was the first activity you learned in the barrio. For Mama, we promised to start fresh, but little did we know that The Gangster had declared a "green light" on Angelica's sons.

Landing her job at Bright Wood, a mill that manufactured everything from bi-fold doors to staircase components, gave Mama a badly needed boost in self-confidence. She dived into her work, sorting and grading pine lumber as if she worked for Jesus Himself. She took her job at Bright Wood as confirmation that God was directing her, and she immediately found daycare for my two little brothers.

At our Madras schools, we older boys were expected to "blend in" to the white culture, and it affected each of us differently. My younger brother and I adapted pretty well at first. We had never seen so many white people crammed into one place before. I was determined to fit in and make friends quickly, but at the junior high school, my older brother ran into trouble.

"I didn't fight back, Mama," he said after his first day at school. Mama searched his determined dark eyes, heartbroken. His mouth was bloody and one eye swollen. The shirt that Mama had so carefully laid out for him that morning was stained and torn. A hopeless expression crossed her face, then anger. It dawned upon her that The Gangster refused to let her son live in peace, even hundreds of miles from Vaughn Street. He wanted them back in *his* barrio.

"I tried, Mama, but I can't just let them beat me up." Emotion cracked my brother's voice.

"He can't let them punk (take advantage of) him, Mama!" my younger brother yelled.

She looked at all three of us, reading the same outrage that welled up inside her. She bowed her head a moment before attending to my little brothers, who were crying again.

"Go wash up," she said, and began dishing up beans and rice on our plates.

The futures of my two brothers began curdling like sour milk those first days in Madras. My older brother brawled six or more times the next week to prove that the "California" Mexican wasn't a coward. After school each day, my younger brother soaked up every detail, every punch, as if the painful account nourished his mind. In the years to come, he would emulate his big brother, including joining the Pacoima Vaughn Street Gang. He was Chicano, and no one would ever punk him either.

Twisted Loyalties

"Hey, you wanna go smoke?"

I was terrified that Mama might find out, and often I refused, but not this time. It was summer, hot and boring. Today I missed my barrio, my culture and my *home*

Drive By

in Pacoima. It seemed that we had been kidnapped and lived on a different planet, among aliens, where their culture didn't make any sense. My two little brothers adapted easily. My mother searched out common ground with friends at church, but the three of us older boys pined for the deep bonds we had with Grandmother, uncles, aunts and cousins. I had found a few friends in the neighborhoods, but none were homies that I trusted.

My brothers always found a way to turn this "culture shock" into a challenge to their manhood. They were learning to survive on this violent White Man's turf, and planned on leaving for Pacoima with their new skills just as soon as they could. While sitting cross-legged on the floor, passing around a scraggly marijuana joint, we talked about home: Grandmother, the games we used to play and gangsters. There had been police sweeps "harassing" our barrio, designed by authorities to lock up the veterano gang-bangers who committed the most serious crimes. Friends had been swept up in raids, and my brothers wanted to get back to the action.

"What about Mama?" I asked.

"She'll be okay," my younger brother said. "The barrio needs us, man."

It was a constant fight for Mama to keep my brothers in check while working long hours, sometimes holding down two jobs, and caring for her two youngest. She did her best to keep us in church, but our home became a battleground over gang behavior like shaved heads, tattoos or trash talk. She knew the halls of the school as well as we did, visiting the principal often about their fighting. My younger brother molded himself into a smaller, tougher image of our big brother, and they both considered themselves Pacoima gangsters, even in Madras.

My vow to reject gang life had matured, but I loved my brothers and felt as much like an outsider as they did. They respected my choices, and in the depths of their hearts, they knew that Mama and I were right to start life over. Still, they thought their destinies were entwined with their homies in Pacoima. Often they visited Grandmother, and eventually, their twisted loyalties delivered them back to the Pacoima Vaughn Street Gang.

Fresh Purpose

I Samuel 16:7: "...man looketh on the outward appearance, but the Lord looketh on the heart."

At Living Hope Christian Center, I stood out like a jalapeno pepper in a fruit salad. I had been invited to their youth group, and I wore my gang persona, a guise that kept people from getting too close. In my mind, I kissed off the "love" they showed, thinking that it was just the churchy way everyone acted inside the building. Very few people I knew lived the Christian life outside in the real world.

Strange things had been happening in Pacoima. I heard that my uncles and aunts were leaving the gangs and attending Grandmother's church. If it were true, maybe this "Jesus" that Mama lived for was more interesting than I thought, but I doubted that I would find Him at a Madras youth group. A man dressed in Levis and a tucked-in, checkered shirt was organizing games, and I crossed my arms and slouched back in a chair. I had been churched all my life, and heard every sermon that there was, but not from Josh Gering.

This white guy made sense, and I suddenly hungered to know more of what God had to say to me. I began attending Living Hope with my mother and brothers, and in the following months, Jesus used Josh to break The Gangster's hold over me. Josh was a hardcore Christ Veterano, and he hammered my brain until I welcomed Jesus' gentle voice, just for relief. The Holy Spirit made His home in my heart over time, stripping away my gang disguise and creating a new heart inside me. El Diablo fled like a whipped barrio puppy.

I wasn't perfect after my encounter with Jesus. I still had a vice to deal with: marijuana. And my brothers still drew me into their "clique" sometimes, but over time, God replaced my need to "belong" with a longing to serve my Creator. By 14 years old, I had given my life fully to Christ, and my whole family knew I *belonged* to Him.

"Hey, man, you want to know Jesus Christ?" I was visiting another church in Oregon, and after the service, I stood in the foyer, drinking in the warmth of fellowship. Three young men in slacks and tucked-in polo shirts targeted the "Mexican" dressed "loose," and wearing earrings. When I told them that I served Jesus with my whole heart, they seemed confused.

"You're a few years too late," I laughed, and grabbed one of their hands.

They were Christian brothers, and they didn't even know it. Were they disappointed that they missed a chance to see a "gangsta'" get saved? Maybe they should go where the real gangsters lived, out on the streets in Pacoima.

God was slowly affirming that my mission field lay with youngsters who didn't know their powerful Creator. I wanted boys and girls to know that they could trust Jesus to watch their backs, like He had for me. Jesus would protect them better than any gang. Should I go back to Pacoima and give this message to my barrio family?

God seemed to be saying to me, *Stay put.* But where were the kids that needed the message of hope the Holy Spirit had so clearly spoken to my heart?

Finding Miracles

Psalms 139:8: "If I ascend up into heaven, thou art there; If I make my bed in hell, behold, thou art there."

"I tell you, man, they unloaded their clip right at me, and I was ten #%* feet away! I don't know how they missed!" My younger brother seemed barely aware that he had experienced a miracle from God.

"Jesus did it, man. God has a plan for you, bro." I grinned, shaking my head and thanking God for sending angels to keep my brother alive until he broke down and gave his life to Christ.

Then El Diablo threw my family a wicked curveball. My brother went to *prison.*

When Mama and I read my younger brother's letters from the penitentiary, our hearts ached, and we prayed for a miracle to happen in his soul. We knew that Jesus lives in prisons, too, and that He would spend time with

Drive By

my brother in his cell, during his lonely hours. As the months passed, we noticed a change in the tone of my brother's letters as God showed him a new way of looking at life. His heart, so mangled by past hurts, was beginning to heal.

In the meantime, after being a Christian for years, I needed my own miracle. I was fully absorbed in pursuing an architectural degree in Eugene, when God had to remind me of my first calling: *Snatching youth from The Gangster's house.* The Holy Spirit got my attention when my finances began to dry up for class tuition. It seemed that the harder I worked, the farther behind I got, and my mind seemed restless and edgy, like I was stumbling through rival gang territory.

After months of prayer and reflection, I packed my bags and headed home to Madras. I sought counsel from pastors at Living Hope, and offered to help with their youth outreach, praying that God would confirm what He wanted me to do. Wasn't the next logical step Bible college? I took a job at a mill where I endured a steady stream of "redneck" trash talk, and prayed for quitting time everyday. I knew that God was teaching me patience, but for how *long?* And always in my heart, those penetrating unmistakable words from the Holy Spirit saying, *Prepare.*

One day, Pastor McCloud called me in for a talk. "We've been praying about it, and we feel that you should start an internship here at Living Hope. You'll learn youth ministry from the ground up, John. What do you think?"

I reveled in the peace and fulfillment of being in the center of God's will as I dove into the internship program at Living Hope. I enrolled in the Berean Bible courses, but I still longed to "take the war to the enemy" and put my life experience to work. The Gangster was at work here on the Madras streets, too, and these young people were his prey.

One day, a friend mentioned that a job was opening up where he was employed. "You interested in working at the Boys and Girls Club? It's just part-time. You know, herding around kids, helping plan activities, etc."

The idea hit me between the eyes. I lost no time in getting an interview, and I was IN! Now to figure out how to pay the bills.

"Lord, if this is Your will, help me fill up the other half of my work day." Another friend put me to work, installing flooring with him in the mornings. God was providing and fulfilling my greatest desire to serve Him. I now worked with kids from several ethnic groups who struggled with the very problems that I had worked through, the need to *belong*, fear of the streets, broken trust and broken family, and I understood how these kids thought.

"Hey, how's the virgin?" my older brother jibed as I walked into Mama's living room. He had moved to Madras for a time. (Good-natured trash talk is part of my family's lifestyle, especially anyone associated with the street gangs.)

"I'm blessed, bro," I returned, and I meant it.

My burden for disadvantaged children had grown more intense during the months I worked at the Boys and Girls Club, and miracles unfolded *one day at a time* as I gained favor with the staff. I loved mentoring children: shooting hoops in the gymnasium, or just talking with them about their lives. When a full-time administrative position opened up, I applied, a little hesitant in

Drive By

my step of faith, but God met my need for confidence. I was appointed as the Program Director of the Boys and Girls Club in Madras.

Miracles just keep coming! Mama works for Social Services in Madras. She prepares traditional Mexican meals for friends and family in her kitchen in the home that she *owns*. Since her youth, Mama's prayers have been battering down the house of The Gangster. My youngest brothers, now teenagers, love Jesus, and my grandmother has moved away from Vaughn Street. Grandmother still opens up her home to family and friends who need her loving counsel. Most of my extended family in Pacoima have turned away from gang life and are finding Jesus, "...the friend that sticketh closer than a brother." Proverbs 18:24

Often, I see kids watching MTV or listening to filthy rap music, and I feel like I'm watching someone dig a grave. They say, "I wanna be a gansta. I gotta get tough."

But I *know* that life. I gently tell them that the gang-banger wears a mask and his trash talk covers up the fear inside. I tell them that my older brother is a gangster still, and he says that the toughest gang-banger you meet is the one most afraid. Sometimes I see a flicker of understanding in their eyes, but they usually won't break, not yet. Still, I have planted a seed in their young hearts, and the Holy Spirit will help it grow.

Coming from the Pacoima barrio has taught me to think "out of the box." I know that we are deceived by what a man looks like on the outside. God looks past our clothes, our hair, our skin color, *our sin,* and answers our deepest need. The Holy Spirit has given me a new barrio, and is teaching me that I can trust Him every waking moment. I must see people the way He does, and sacrifice my machismo (pride) to show others His powerful love.

Long after those stormy first years in Madras, Mama refuses to leave any of my brothers in The Gangster's house. In prayer, she lifts them up to Jesus, and waits for Him to fulfill the promise to her in scripture: "Train up a child in the way he should go, and when he is old, he will not depart from it." Proverbs 22:6

It breaks her heart to see the mayhem in their lives, prison, violence, drugs and broken relationships. But while they live, Mama believes that she holds their souls in an iron grip through intercessory prayer. And because of God's mercy, I have joined her.

Dug Out of a Hole

Gary Buss' story
as told by Peggy Thompson

"Come on, Gary! You're gonna miss it!"

Grandpa nudged me with the toe of his boot as I burrowed myself deeper into my sleeping bag. Then I remembered!

"Okay, Grandpa. I'm hurrying."

It was dark as pitch in the tent, and I had to scramble to get dressed. I was feeling around for my other shoe when Grandpa opened the flap of the tent and said softly, "Let's go."

We walked outside into the cold, fresh air and I heard him say, "In the morning light, I meet God."

My grandpa had promised to show me my first sunrise, and I was beside myself with excitement. "Is it starting, Grandpa?" I asked impatiently, as I stared hard out into the vast darkness.

"Shhh, Gary."

Neither of us said a word after that.

We stood side by side, the old man and the young boy, and watched a blazing glow slowly start to rise behind the tall, jagged peaks in the east. It took my breath away as a huge, golden backdrop formed behind the peaks, those dark and silent giants of the night. The glow rose higher and higher until it seemed to crown them with a halo, and then it suddenly burst forth, spilling over onto the land. Sun-kissed rocks in hues of red, orange and gold surrounded me. It was glorious.

It was my first camping trip. I was 7, and it was just Grandpa and I. We were in Nevada, the high desert, and I thought it was beautiful in its starkness.

Grandpa and I had many outdoor adventures together. We would get up at daylight and fish in a little stream that you could jump across, and he taught me how to catch brook trout that he cooked for our breakfast. He showed me my first rattlesnake and taught me how to respect them and protect myself. We would scour the rocks together, and as I would find petrified wood and agates, Grandpa told me what they were and how they were formed. It was because of my special times with him that I developed such a passion for rocks. He was the great mentor in my life.

At night, after a long and exciting day exploring, we would climb into our sleeping bags, and I would chatter my head off about the excitements of the day while Grandpa was trying to go to sleep. I remember once I asked him, "Grandpa, do you believe in angels?"

"Of course, Gary. In fact, if you close your eyes and lay very still, sometimes you can just barely feel the flutter of their wings on your cheeks as they watch over you."

Instantly, I closed my eyes and waited to feel this sensation, but I ended up falling asleep.

When I was in my late teens and early 20s, I began to pursue my interest in rocks, and as I learned more and more about them, my passion grew. A friend of mine had a similar interest and he and I began going on trips together. Unfortunately, I lost my friend, Jake, to a heart attack. After my grandpa, I always considered Jake my mentor.

After awhile, I had the good fortune to meet another rock hound, Dan, and we started going rock hunting together.

In the summer of 1982, Dan and I planned a three-week rock-hounding trip to Wildcat Mountain in Oregon. I was 38 years old. When the day finally arrived, I woke up early, as excited as a kid. Beckie, my wife, was cooking breakfast as I pulled on my faded jeans, long-sleeved, plaid shirt, heavy socks and hiking boots.

The wonderful aroma of frying bacon filled the air, and I hurried to finish shaving. My stomach growled a little, and I had to laugh at my voracious appetite. We had eaten a light supper the night before, and I intended to do some serious eating at breakfast.

I made my way to the kitchen where I quietly lingered for a moment, leaning against the door jam with my arms crossed across my chest. My heart swelled with love as I watched my wife standing at the stove, carefully turning the sizzling bacon over in the frying pan. My mind quickly flashed back to when we first met. I was 22 and a good friend of mine arranged a blind date for us. We hit it off immediately. It wasn't too long before we decided to get married. As far as I was concerned, this was another of God's miracles.

Her voice startled me. "I know you're there, Gary. Don't think you're going to sneak up on me," she teased.

I laughed and crossed the room to where she was standing. "Think you're pretty smart, huh?" Wrapping both arms around her from behind, I pulled her close to me and started nuzzling her neck. Her long, auburn hair hung in soft waves and its silkiness brushed my face. I knew this loving gesture of mine tickled her and she started to wriggle in my arms.

"Gary! I'm trying to cook your breakfast!" She giggled, turned her head and gave me a quick kiss on the tip of my nose. "Could you hand me that plate, hon?"

"How come you always know when I come into the room?" I asked, as I took the plate from the countertop and handed it to her.

"Your aftershave gives you away." She laughed at

Dug Out of a Hole

the expression on my face.

"You'd make a great detective," I retorted, as I leaned down and opened the oven door just a bit. "Umm. Cinnamon rolls. You're going all out this morning, babe," I said gratefully.

Beckie took the rolls out of the oven, put one on her plate and two on mine, which was already piled high with bacon and eggs. As she carried them to the kitchen table, I grabbed the coffee pot. She sat down and I stood, filling her mug with the delicious brew. Then I grabbed mine and poured the dark, steaming coffee, filling it right to the brim.

As I sat down opposite her, I was eager to dig in. With my fork in midair, I hesitated. She was looking intently at me, a little concerned.

"What's wrong?"

"Nothing. Well, it's just that three weeks is a long time, Gary."

"Are you worried or are you going to miss me?" I teased as I grinned at her.

She gave me a quick smile and we both started to eat. I studied her face for a moment. "You're not really worried, are you?"

She squirmed on her chair a bit and then sighed. "I guess not. I'm just a little on edge."

She took a sip of her coffee. "It's just that a lot can happen and I..."

"You *are* worried." Reaching across the table, I took her hand in mine. "Honey, you know I have been rockhounding for years. And Dan and I have been working together for a long time. We know what we're doing. We've planned everything out carefully. Made our lists and even checked them twice."

My attempt at a little humor didn't erase the tiny lines of concern etched on her features. "Please don't worry, babe." I squeezed her hand with reassurance.

She gave me a quick smile. "Oh, all right. But only if you promise to take your guardian angel with you."

"I promise."

We both shared a laugh. I had told Beckie about my grandpa's angel story and we talked and teased about angels occasionally.

Dan and I took off on a very hot and steamy August day in 1982. It was a 150-mile drive from Springfield, where we lived, to Wildcat Mountain. My four-wheel drive pickup pulled a 20-foot camp trailer that was loaded with our groceries and supplies.

Going into Wildcat, the roads were strictly four-wheel drive, very rough terrain. We found a great spot to camp and planned to dig about 400 yards away from that. There was a little place down the hill, by one of the parks, where we would be able to take showers, and we were also close enough to Prineville if we had to go for extra groceries.

We could hardly wait to set up camp so we could get out there with our rock picks, chipping hammers and chisels. And gloves! Without gloves, the rhyolite would scrape the flesh from your hands. We were like two kids in a candy store.

We used a pick, shovel and wheelbarrow, making an open pit, mine-type hole with a tailings pile out one end. It was a long trench and Dan worked at one end and I at the other. When I unearthed my first thunder egg, I just howled with delight. Dan came running and I showed him my find. We both proceeded to happily dig out thunder eggs, the Oregon State rock, and lost track of

Dug Out of a Hole

time in our passion to find more. It was dusk before we decided to stop digging.

"How about if we wrap it up for today?" I asked Dan.

"Steaks and coffee by the campfire, sounds great to me! It's your turn to cook." He laughed as he took a bandana from his hip pocket and wiped some of the sweat and grit from his face.

Later, as we were sitting comfortably by the campfire, I told Dan about some of my wonderful experiences as a small boy with my grandpa.

"Grandpa and I were out together when I found my very first thunder egg. I asked him, 'Grandpa, what's this?' He held up the little round nodule, all bumpy on the outside, and told me it was made from rhyolite and volcanic activity, and when it cooled it filled up with agate on the inside. 'Gary,' Grandpa said, 'when you cut one of these little round balls and see what's inside, you will be the first person to ever see it since it was formed by the Creator. No two are alike. You cut it and polish it and it's really beautiful. It's called a 'thunder egg.'"

While Dan and I dug on Wildcat Mountain, thunderstorms were almost a daily occurrence. We were aware that there were some fires in the surrounding area. Throughout our stay, we watched them work with tankers on a fire on the other side of Mill Creek, several miles away, across the canyon. The Bureau of Land Management had choppers in the air checking the progress of all current fires and also looking for any others that might have started.

The night before our last day, there was a huge thunderstorm with hail about the size of quarters. The next morning when we walked up to the hole, we had to shovel the hail out of it before we could start closing it up. Closing up a hole for safety reasons was a responsibility of all rock-hounders and, of course, we also didn't want anyone else to find our treasure. By noon, we had managed to get the hole filled to within 10-12 feet of the top.

"Hey, Dan, let's take a break." Perspiration was running down my neck and my back and I was hungry.

"Okay, but don't expect me to come to your place. I'm too hot and tired."

We shared a laugh. Reaching out, I dragged a five-gallon bucket filled with thunder eggs toward me for a seat, and there I plopped as I started peeling back the plastic wrap on a sandwich.

As I munched, I heard a slight noise behind me that got my attention, and in my peripheral vision, I saw moving earth. Instinctively I jumped up, but I was too late. In that split second, I was covered in total darkness. I couldn't move. I couldn't breathe. What I didn't know was that the upper side of the hill had collapsed and buried me completely. A half-ton boulder had landed on the left side of my chest, and it had thrown me into the wall on the right side, which shattered that side of my face.

"Oh, God! I'm coming, Gary!"

Danny was hollering above me. I could hear the sound of his pick as he frantically dug into the dirt. The silliest idea came to me: *I'm not going to die from being buried. I'm going to die from being hit in the head by Dan with his pick.*

It didn't take Dan long to unearth my head. "Oh, God, Gary! I'll get you out! Hang on!" He was beside himself with anxiety.

But with all his digging he could only get down to

my waist. My body was in an upright, slanted position and the lower portion was down too far for him to get me out without the rest of the hillside coming down.

There was no way I could tell what my injuries were, but I knew they were pretty bad. My face and mouth were bleeding heavily, and I kept gasping for air. I just couldn't breathe. There was no feeling from my neck down to my waist.

"Dan," I managed to gasp. "Go for help!"

"No! I can't leave you here like this!"

Struggling for more air, I managed to tell him, "We are the only people on the mountain! We...need...help!"

It was true. We hadn't seen another person the entire three weeks we were up there. There was a mile of hiking on the rough road to the campground and another three miles to get to the main spur road that led off the mountain to the highway. Then it took almost an hour of driving to get to Prineville. There was a forest service station on the way, but it was hardly ever manned.

Dan's gaze locked with mine and our silent, meaningful exchanges spoke volumes about the situation we were in.

He turned away abruptly and started off in the direction of help, wherever and whatever that would be. I was alone, encased in dirt and barely able to breathe.

The air was heavy with silence. It seemed surreal. My right eye was swelling shut, but I managed to look around at the tall, green pine trees surrounding the area and said, "God, I don't know anyone who loves life more than I do, but if this is my time, I'm ready."

My survival instinct kicked in, and I just knew if I closed my eyes, I wasn't going to open them again. As I lay there trying to keep my eyes open and my mind active, I quoted some scripture verses to myself that I had learned from a class I had been taking.

Dan had gone about one and a half miles down the trail when he found two hikers.

"Please, please! We need help!" He explained what had happened, that he was going for help, and asked if they would be willing to go up to the diggings and stay with me.

The young woman spoke right up. "I'm a registered nurse. You bet we will!"

The sound of voices and approaching footsteps made me wonder if Dan had already found help. Was God answering my prayers? Then this young couple just seemed to appear out of nowhere.

The woman took over immediately. "Hi, Gary. I'm Helen and I'm a registered nurse." She locked her gaze with mine and added, "We're going to get you out of here and get you the medical attention you need."

The impact of her words overwhelmed me. Registered nurse? God had put a registered nurse there for me? At just the right place and at just the right time? A calm, serene feeling began to fill my heart, and as I looked at Helen's face, I thought that must be what an angel looked like. She had very short, wispy, platinum blond hair that framed her heart-shaped face. Her clear, blue eyes were steady and compassionate.

Before long, there was a flurry of activity. The Oregon State Police, the Forest Service, the Sheriff's Department, almost anyone who had anything to do with anything showed up. I smiled inside myself. "Dan sure sent the troops!" He had stopped at the forest station to see if, by chance, someone was there and whether there was an active phone. Because of the thunderstorms and fires, the Bureau of Land Management had spotters manning the station that day.

Then the ambulance arrived. They brought a litter over to where I was and everything became a blur for me. But I could hear voices. Most of the time it was Helen's, soft but filled with authority.

As they eased me onto the litter, they decided they would transport me out of the area in an ambulance.

"Absolutely not!" I heard her say. "His blood pressure is very low and he's bleeding internally. Let's get some pressure cuffs on his legs and pump them up to keep more of the blood in the upper part of his body. And we need to bring his blood pressure up."

"Ma'am, he needs to get to a hospital."

"You will never get him off this mountain alive in an ambulance. The road is too rough. You would have to pack him down from the diggings about a half mile and it's a very steep, rocky road. A four-wheel drive couldn't even manage that. You need to airlift him out." She hovered over me, she insisted, cajoled and absolutely took charge of the situation. No one had a better solution.

Because of the fact that the BLM had helicopters flying around for fire control purposes, they were able to get in touch with one of the pilots and he said he would come in. This guy really had to know what he was doing because the only possible landing site around was a little meadow surrounded by tall ponderosa pines just below us. It was just big enough to let you know it was there. There was no doubt in my mind that God guided that chopper down to a safe landing in the meadow.

Before I knew it, I was being loaded onto the chopper. Helen supervised.

"Be careful, please! I am positive he has broken ribs and probably a punctured lung."

Since it was just a little two-seat smoke jumper, they had to take the doors off both sides to get the litter inside. My head stuck out one door and my feet out the other. Helen crawled in and straddled the litter so I wouldn't fall out either side when the pilot had to make turns.

The chopper landed in the parking lot of the Prineville Hospital three hours after the accident. A team of doctors was standing by to receive me. Inside the emergency room, the doctor shared a few brief words.

"The reason you are having a hard time breathing, Gary, is because the left side of your chest is crushed and the left lung has been collapsed." He further explained that he was going to have to insert a tube to re-inflate the lung. "This is going to hurt a bit."

They didn't have time to clean me up or give me an anesthetic. The doctor made an incision, pried my ribs open and attached the tube to my collapsed lung.

"Call my wife. Please, would someone call my wife? I would like to have her here with me."

They got the information and Beckie's work phone number from Dan. Not wanting to panic her, they called and told her I had been in an accident, was having x-rays, and that I wanted her to come to the Prineville Hospital.

Beckie drove to Prineville only to discover that, after getting me stabilized and supported medically, they had transported me by ambulance to St. Charles Medical Center in Bend.

The Prineville Hospital told her I had been transferred, and gave her my wallet and bloody clothes.

Dug Out of a Hole

"Would you like to talk to the attending physician, Mrs. Buss?"

"No, thank you. I need to drive for another 30 minutes to Bend, and I don't want to drive any more upset than I am already."

Discussion was swirling all around me. "In all likelihood, there has been head trauma. We'll have to see how soon we can get him to surgery." They took more x-rays and discussed my spine and broken back.

When my wife arrived at St. Charles, the attending nurse went out into the hall to talk to her before letting her in my room.

"Please prepare yourself, Mrs. Buss. There are a lot of issues here. The x-rays from Prineville show a broken back, collapsed lung, brain injury, and his pelvis has been separated from the spinal column. There are also crushed vertebrae in his neck. The orbit bone below his right eye is shattered, and you will see for yourself that he can't focus with that eye. We are still assessing internal injuries, but he will probably have brain surgery tonight. If he survives the night, he will undoubtedly be a quadriplegic."

Beckie entered my room with more than a little trepidation. She walked quickly to my bedside and gently lifted my right hand to her lips. Her eyes glistened with tears. She gazed at my broken, still dirty body covered with grit, tubes coming in and going out of me everywhere, and my mess of a face with that blood-red eye that I couldn't control.

"Hi, honey. I'm sure sorry to put you through this."

"Oh, Gary. You look horrible. I just didn't expect to see you like this. They didn't tell me much of anything until just a couple of minutes ago."

Swallowing the lump in my throat, I croaked, "I love you, honey. I am so sorry."

"Shhh." She gently put the tip of her forefinger to my battered and swollen lips. "I want you to know there was a comforting presence with me as I drove to get here. I just can't explain it, but I know you are going to come through this just fine."

There was a swishing sound as the door to my room opened and a nurse came in. "It's been five minutes, Mrs. Buss. That's all you can have right now."

As soon as Beckie stepped outside the Intensive Care Unit, there were three pastors waiting, who had come to pray with her.

A local pastor also showed up. "I just can't leave you here with no place to stay and to be all alone to face this. I have arranged for a home you can stay in."

As it turned out, this pastor knew a couple who had a home that they opened up for missionaries and visiting pastors to stay in while they were in Bend. It had a downstairs apartment complex with two bedrooms, a living room, a kitchen, laundry and its own entry. They were involved in the Gideon Society whose mission is to give out Bibles. They were wonderful to Beckie and supplied her every need. "We only have a few rules here," they told her. "Everything in this house is yours. Just lock the door when you leave and don't replace anything." It was a real blessing to know that my wife was being so well taken care of.

The rest of my injuries consisted of 37 fractures to my ribs, none of which were in tact and some even had multiple fractures. A rib had punctured the cardiac sac of the heart and looked like it had bruised it, which would explain why my heart was beating in weird rhythms. My liver was acting funny so they kept a close eye on that. My pelvis was separated from the spinal column, and only time would tell if I would get feeling back. There was a long road of recuperation ahead of me.

I had a lot of time on my hands and I did a lot of heavy thinking. The thing I thought about the most was when both Beckie and I gave our hearts to the Lord. As a young boy, I was raised in the Catholic Church. I believed there was a God, a Creator, and I felt He was someone I could run to whenever I was in trouble. Neither Beckie nor I had a personal relationship with the Lord until 1970. That's when God stepped into our lives and seemed to say, "I'm tired of waiting on you guys so I'm going to grab some Christian people and put them into your life." And He did.

People at work started sharing their faith with me. A good friend of mine returned from Vietnam. He was heavy into drugs and was a terrible "meltdown" case. I had grown up with him and we ran wild together for a long time. One night, he, his girlfriend, Beckie and I went to see the movie *The Cross and The Switchblade*. We had dinner together afterward and they both gave us their testimonies. God even used my insurance agent, who belonged to an Assembly of God Church in Eugene. He started sharing and inviting us to church. The process took many months, but on November 10, 1970, we went to the altar at church and gave our hearts to the Lord.

Being a Christian is all about relationships, especially the one you have with the Lord. I reflected upon how blessed we were that God intervened in our lives when He did because it was His strength and love I drew upon during the accident and its aftermath.

The other thing that consumed my thoughts during

my long recovery was the registered nurse, Helen, who was with me from the scene of the accident until I was safely delivered into professional hands for treatment. Then she just seemed to vanish into thin air. I remembered asking her once where she worked, and I thought she said at a hospital on the coast. Tracking down Helen became our number one priority as soon as I was well enough to get around. She had saved my life.

As soon as I was able, which was about three months later, we made a trip to the coast and stopped at the hospital. We were told there was no one on the staff by the name Helen Cooper. When we returned home from that trip, we got a call from someone in administration at that hospital. That person told us there had been someone by that name who used to work there, but she had moved to Central Oregon. We made trips to Central Oregon, but we never found Helen. Driving home from our last trip, Beckie and I decided that Helen had to have been an angel sent by God in my great time of need.

It took a very long time to recover from the accident, but I am absolutely amazed that I can walk, talk, hunt, fish and play golf, when I should have been a quadriplegic. In fact, six weeks after returning home, I sang in a concert at Willamette Christian Center in Eugene. Some of the guys in my section had to prop me up, and I didn't have enough breath yet to hold the notes as long as I should have, but I did it!

After the concert, I sat quietly in a chair with my eyes closed to rest a bit. Within a few seconds, I was positive I felt little fluttering sensations on my cheeks. "Thanks, Helen," I murmured softly.

Losing a Child

Jim and Becky Leach's story
as told by Melanie Widmer

Today would have been my son's 3rd birthday. But on this hot, still August day, there won't be a party on the lawn, no balloons, no presents and no cake with tiny, plastic dinosaurs. On this painful anniversary, this birthday-not-to-be, I sit alone and stare at my ring. Peridot would have been my little boy's birthstone. As the green facets of the stone catch the bright summer sun, I think back to the beginning of this bittersweet journey.

My husband, Jim, and I always wanted a houseful of kids. Jim would have been happy to start trying for children as soon as we were married. He grew up in a big family (six boys!) and loved all the noise and activity, but I convinced him to wait a few years. I thought we needed a little time for just the two of us before we expanded our family. Even so, as youth pastors, our home was always full of kids — just not our own.

Finally, after three years of marriage, in early 2002, we were in a place where we both felt ready to raise a child. Hopefully, expectantly, we stopped using birth control. This was it. We were starting a family!

During the next few months, it became increasingly difficult not to obsess about having a baby. Every month, I would count forward forty weeks to calculate the due date of the baby we prayed for. But things were not going well. So many of our friends had gotten pregnant as soon as they started trying, or even when they weren't trying at all. What was wrong with me?

Month after fruitless month we rode a horrible roller coaster. We would begin optimistically, but then each month was like we were going through the five stages of grief. First was denial (Maybe we took the pregnancy test too early, or maybe it's a false negative.), then anger (Why are high school girls getting pregnant, and I can't?

Losing a Child

It's just a cruel irony.), then bargaining (God, we promise to be the best parents we can possibly be if You'll just give us this baby.), then sadness (Am I broken? What if we can't have children?), and finally, acceptance (Okay, next month, we'll try again.).

After seven frustrating months, we took a trip south to Klamath Falls to visit our friends, John and Kola. It was there on a Sunday night that God began the work that would change our lives.

We attended church with John and Kola, and afterward we lingered to pray at the altar. The pastor, whom we didn't know well, came up to us and what he said gave us back the hope we were beginning to lose.

"The Lord showed me you are trying to get pregnant, but there is something wrong with Becky's body. I'm going to pray that God will heal you."

He did pray, and we were truly touched and knew this was the turning point. Later, when we got into the car to return home with our friends, Jim asked John if he had said anything to anyone about our wanting to have a child. He said they hadn't.

The following month, November, I took yet another pregnancy test. I picked up the test and saw what I had been praying to see all these months: two lines. We were having a baby!

Christmas that year was so full of joy. We couldn't wait to let our families in on our happiness. We broke the good news by giving our parents little bibs that said, "I love my Grandpa" and "I love my Grandma." Everyone was so excited for us and couldn't wait until I had the big pregnant belly and they could feel the baby kick.

As the year wound down, we were about to fall from the heights of euphoria to the depths of despair, which would take us months to swim out of. January 1st would be the worst day of our lives.

Before dawn on New Years Day, I woke up with a piercing pain in my abdomen. It was so excruciating. I was about to wake Jim when the room suddenly brightened. I really can't explain that light (the sun hadn't yet risen), but I do know I felt an amazing peace. It was like God just gathered me into His arms and held me there until I fell back to sleep.

In the morning, I tried to hold on to that peace, but a feeling of dread was starting to creep in. I went into the bathroom and saw way too much blood. There was no longer any question. I had miscarried our baby.

The hardest thing I've ever done was to tell Jim we lost our child. He desperately wanted children. He was so ready to be a father. I think he had been ready his whole life. The news devastated him. He held me for a long time and we both wept until we ran out of tears.

Jim was very caring and supportive during those first terrible days, but nothing could really ease my grief.

Telling our families that the baby was gone was hard, but at least they could mourn with us. The harder part was just going about our normal, busy lives. None of our friends, and no one in our congregation at Living Hope Christian Center, had known that we were pregnant, and the pain was just too raw and personal to confide in anyone else about the miscarriage.

Even Jim and I couldn't bring ourselves to talk with each other about what had happened. Speaking about our loss just seemed to rip the wound open wider. We were both lost in a fog of grief that no one else could see. The fog kept us isolated from everyone and from

Losing a Child

each other. I often found myself in the room that would have been the nursery. I would hold the stuffed lamb that had been a gift for our baby from Jim's mom. I listened to the lamb play "Jesus loves me" over and over, and asked, "Does He? Does Jesus really love me?"

We both felt abandoned by God. This child had been the desire of our hearts, something we had looked forward to our entire lives. Too soon after we were given this gift, it was ripped away from us. Had God really healed my body just to take away the child we finally conceived?

As crushed as we were, it was God who pulled us through. It was to God whom we poured out our anger and pain. He took our despair and gave us healing. Through the darkness, we held onto Psalm 62:8: "Trust in Him at all times, O people; Pour out your hearts to Him, for God is our refuge." And He was.

After many weeks, the fog of grief began to lift. As desperately as we missed our baby, we could finally begin to accept that he was in heaven, and we could be with him one day.

Jim and I both believed that our baby was a boy. We named him Christian James Leach.

We knew we had to say goodbye to Christian, but vowed never to forget him. I wrote him a letter and bought a ring with his birthstone that I still wear, in his memory. Jim bought a poster for the nursery with a picture of Jesus with a child in His arms, so we will always remember where our little boy is.

In March, we were attending the Northwest Intercessors Conference in Portland when the minister, Phil Pringle, started speaking on a topic that struck us like an arrow. He himself had lost a child, and God had given him a special gift to pray for couples that were having trouble having children. He had prayed for many couples that were then healed of barrenness and other reproductive problems. Of course, we ran straight down to the altar for prayer. Almost immediately after being prayed for, I fell to the floor. It wasn't so much that I was knocked over as much as that I could no longer stand. God's power was just too much to stand up under. As I laid there on the carpet, I could hear the soft worship music and people praying all around me, but mostly I was aware of warmth like electricity surging through my body. As much as I feared to hope for it, I knew that God had finally healed me.

A Bible verse from Philippians came to my mind, "He that began a good work in you will be faithful to complete it." I know God is faithful, and He was completing His good work in our lives.

A month later it was time to take the first pregnancy test since we had lost Christian. I woke up early, anxious to find out if we were at last going to be parents. I took the test and closed my eyes. I counted the heartbeats in my ears until it was time to peek. I opened my eyes and, sure enough, there were two pink lines. I got down on my knees on the fuzzy bathroom rug and prayed that God would keep this baby healthy. I didn't think we could bear to lose this child, too.

I took the test into the kitchen where Jim was making coffee. "I'm pregnant!" I said, and handed him the plastic stick. He just stared at it without reacting for a moment. Then he hugged me and said how happy he was.

For the next several weeks, we were both cautiously excited. We missed the unguarded exuberance we felt

Losing a Child

during my first pregnancy, but we were afraid to celebrate too much in case something went wrong again.

As fear lingered in my heart, God led me to a verse, Psalm 139, which I held onto as a personal prayer and promise for this child.

"God, I pray You would knit this baby together in my womb. I pray that Your eyes will watch over this unformed body. I pray that You would create this baby into Your wonderful creation, and I thank You that You have planned the days ahead for this baby before one of them came to be."

In June, it was time for our first ultrasound. Jim and I walked hand in hand into the reception area at Mountain View Hospital. We were excited to see this first fuzzy picture of our baby, but also terrified that the doctor might reveal some problem. It seemed like it took forever for the nurse to call us back into the exam room. Finally, it was our turn. A nurse tech greeted us and had me hop up on the exam table. She asked us if we were ready to see our baby. You bet we were! She rubbed that cold, clear, jelly-like stuff on my belly, and as she moved the sensor over me, there he was on the monitor. We saw for the first time the tiny arms and legs and sweet little profile. Our doctor reassured us that we had made it through the most dangerous time of pregnancy, and the chances were good that I would carry this baby to term.

Jim and I felt like we had both been holding our breath for the past three months, and now we could at last exhale. From that day on, we felt like we could fully embrace the experience. We could finally let go and believe that God was blessing us with this child.

On Father's Day, Jim was making some announcements during the service at our church, when he slipped in our own little "announcement." He said, "We've been hearing a rumor going around that my wife and I are going to have a baby. Well... it's true."

The entire congregation erupted in cheers and applause. Everyone was so happy for us, but no one was happier than Jim and I.

The baby grew through the rest of the year and so did I. Never had it been so much fun to gain so much weight! I loved being able to feel the new life growing inside of me.

We spent the autumn of that year decorating the nursery. We both love Africa, so we chose that as our theme, painting the room blue and green and incorporating palm trees and lots of animals.

Our church threw us a baby shower, but really it was more of a baby downpour than a shower. Everyone blessed us so much. We ended up with more baby gear than we knew what to do with. Afterward, as Jim and I sorted through all the receiving blankets, onesies and stuffed animals, we could really see a bit of scripture playing out in our lives. There's a song from the 1990s, based on a portion of the book of Isaiah. The chorus goes like this: "He gives beauty for ashes, strength for fear, gladness for mourning, peace for despair."

God had done all of that for us, and the joy in that revelation made us both stop and praise the Lord again, standing in our African nursery, surrounded by gifts representing the love and good wishes of our friends and family.

On January 30, 2004, we welcomed Jonathon James Leach into the world. I can't even describe the unspeakable joy of holding this child for the first time. This child that we had longed for, prayed for and agonized over. His hair was so blonde you could hardly see it, and his eyes were impossibly blue. This was our son!

And now our story has come full circle. Now, in August 2006, Jonathon is 2 1/2 years old, and he is the light of our lives. We found out on Valentine's Day that we were going to have another baby. (That was the best Valentine's present ever!) I'm seven months pregnant, and a little uncomfortable, but mostly very happy on this hot, still August day. Life for our growing family is good. Jim just took Jonathon to get some ice cream (as a reward for being such a good boy and picking up his toys), and I'm taking these few, rare moments of solitude to remember the child who slipped away, and to praise God for the child we have and for the children to come.

He gives gladness for the mourning, peace for despair.

From Panic to Peace

Patricia Woll's story
as told by Peggy Thompson

We were having lasagna for dinner, which was Jack's favorite. Opening the oven door with a potholder, I slid the dish carefully onto the rack. Just as I was shutting the door, Leila toddled up to me and reached out her little hand to touch the stove.

"No, no, Leila! Hot! It's very hot!"

As I leaned down to pick her up, I heard the phone ring. It only rang twice so I assumed Jack had answered.

"It's for you, honey," he said as he poked his head into the kitchen. He reached out and offered me the phone.

"Who is it?" Walking toward him, still holding Leila, I wondered who would call us so close to dinnertime.

"Dr. Hunter."

"Our doctor? What in the world?"

Jack lifted Leila out of my arms and retreated to the family room with her.

"Hello?"

"Patty? This is Dr. Hunter. I hope I didn't interrupt your dinner."

"Not at all."

"Patty, you had your annual mammogram taken four days ago…"

An anxious, unsettled feeling started to grow in my stomach.

As I stood in my bright kitchen, my gaze momentarily wandered, taking in the splashes of red and yellow that made it so cheerful and warm. I felt happy and safe in this room.

I tried to listen carefully, but at the same time, I was resisting what he was telling me. My hand gripped the phone, tense, tinged with desperation as it all began to register in my mind.

The sound of my own voice sounded very small and helpless. "Okay. I will."

Standing there alone in my modern kitchen, my gaze took in all the things that had been such a big and important part of my life just a few moments ago. The new refrigerator, the way the red mixing bowls stood out against the fresh yellow paint on the wall, the red border on the yellow and white gingham curtains that gave the room such punch.

There was no way I could realize that I was in shock as I wandered out of the kitchen to find my husband. As soon as I entered the family room, he turned his head and fixed his gaze on my face. "Patty? What did the doctor want?"

His voice sounded like it was so far away. It echoed as if he had spoken to me from the end of a tunnel and the sound had bounced off the walls.

Jack got up off the couch and walked over to where I was standing. "Patty? Did you hear me?"

His gaze was riveted on mine, and he took hold of my shoulders. When he touched me, it brought me back to reality somehow. "What? What did you say?"

"What did Dr. Hunter call about? What's wrong?"

"Oh, Jack!" Flinging myself into his arms, I buried my face into his shoulder as I started to sob and tremble. "I have to go to the hospital for a biopsy! My breast... there's something in my mammogram..."

"Mommy's crying," said Minta, our 4-year-old daughter, as she got up from the floor where she had been playing with her dolls. She walked over to where Jack and I were standing. "Please don't cry, Mama."

The next wave hit me. "The children! What will happen to our children?"

Jack had to turn his attention to the girls. Leila was only 18 months old and she had started to cry. Minta was nervously holding onto a fistful of his slacks.

Frantic with terror, I walked to the back door and went outside into the backyard. This can't be happening! This has to be a nightmare!

Leaning against the side of the house for support, my chest was heaving as I gasped for breath between sobs.

Jack took over inside the house. He made sure the lasagna was taken out of the oven. He fed the girls, bathed them and put them to bed while reassuring them that Mama was just fine. "She's just a little upset right now, but she and I are going to talk about it and make it all better." From time to time, he would glance out one of the windows to check on me and to be sure I was still in the yard. When he was finished, it was dusk and he came outside to be with me.

Leading me by the hand, he said, "Come on, Patty. Let's sit on the lawn swing and talk about this, honey."

Our yard was lush and filled with a potpourri of flowers. It was one of my favorite relaxing places. We sat together on the swing in the mild, spring twilight.

"Jack, this can't be happening to me."

"Honey, I would be less than honest if I didn't tell you I'm upset, too. But do we have to think the worst right away?"

"Cancer! We're talking about cancer, Jack!"

"Shhhh." He tried to calm me and wrapped his arm around me. "I know, I know."

"I'm too young."

With one of his hands, he gently turned my face toward his and gazed into my eyes. "Make the appointment right away, Patty. I'll be with you every step of the way."

We sat there together until darkness enveloped us, then walked hand in hand into the house.

Within a couple of days, I had been worked into the breast surgeon's schedule and he did the biopsy. Two days later, I received the phone call that told me everything was fine. The relief I felt was so tremendous that I felt weak in the knees. "I'm going to live! I'm fine!" I went out into the backyard and picked a rose bouquet to put on the dinner table. Then I called Jack at work and told him. We both cried with relief.

My appointment was for 4 p.m. Spotting a parking place reasonably close to the Imaging Center, I parked the Tahoe and counted my blessings because I wouldn't have to run to be on time.

For the past 20 years, I had been very conscientious about having mammograms done yearly.

Seating myself in the waiting room, I glanced at my watch and was pleased to see that it was exactly 4:00. There was a stack of magazines on a table next to my chair, and I reached over and picked one up. I had just begun paging through it when the nurse called my name.

"Mrs. Woll?"

"Right here." Putting the magazine back on the table, I got up from the chair, adjusted the strap on my shoulder bag and followed her back to the dressing rooms.

"I think you know the drill," she smiled at me.

"I sure do," I smiled back.

"Great. When you are changed and ready, just open

the door of your dressing room and I'll take you back.

Following her instructions, she met me right outside my door and we went into the X-ray room. "Four pictures and I'm out of here," I thought to myself.

Before I knew it, she had taken six! It was a little surprising, but not alarming.

"I'll be right back, Mrs. Woll. The radiologist is here right now and if we're lucky, we might be able to get him to look at your film."

"Sure. Thank you." Closing the hospital gown around my body, I found a chair in the room and perched on the edge of it.

A few minutes later, the radiologist stepped into the room with my films. He slapped two of them up on the wall under the clips provided for that purpose.

"Hi. I'm Doctor Grady. See this picture on the left?"

"Yes."

"Well, that's last year's."

Then, with the tip of a pencil, he drew my attention to a particular spot on the film on the right.

"See this area?"

"Yes."

"That little speck wasn't there last year. I don't think it's anything to worry about, but I do think it would be prudent to have a biopsy. Anytime there's a change, it's better to be on the safe side."

"Okay. I understand."

Leaving the Imaging Center and walking to my car, I was calm. Actually, I was serene. There was no fear or concern at all.

On the way home, I couldn't help flashing back 20 years to when I was a young mother, and I absolutely freaked out when I was told I needed a biopsy. That was before I had God in my life. Now that I was in His hands, I felt safe, protected and loved.

When I went to have the biopsy, Jack accompanied me.

They took me into a room where there was a table that had two holes at the top.

"If you will please lay face down, Mrs. Woll..."

"Patty. Please call me Patty. Mrs. Woll sounds so, well, formal."

The nurse gave me a smile. "Okay, Patty. You need to be face down and we have to put your breasts in the two holes."

It took some maneuvering, but when we were done, the table was raised. It was such a ridiculous position, and I found it absolutely hilarious. "I feel like a car getting a lube job," I laughed.

"Patty, you're a breath of fresh air," the nurse commented. "Most women don't react that way." She couldn't keep herself from laughing with me.

After the biopsy, we were getting ready to leave the hospital when the radiologist caught up with us.

"I'm pretty confident that nothing new is there, but we have to make sure."

The next evening he called and he was very upset. "I'm really sorry to tell you this, but it's malignant. There are some calcifications. It's definitely cancer."

Some questions immediately came to mind and I started asking him some of them.

"No, I really can't give you those answers. You need a breast surgeon now."

"Okay."

When I learned from the radiologist that I had cancer, I didn't feel panic, anxiety or fear. My first thought was, "Oh, okay. I guess that's what we're doing now." That's not the typical reaction. Just the word cancer itself scares people.

Turning to Jack, I said, "It's cancer and we need to find a breast surgeon."

A blanket of peace surrounded me as I silently prayed a prayer of faith. "We know we are in Your hands, Lord, and we want to do what You want. I don't want to miss what I am supposed to learn in this, and I want You to be glorified throughout the whole thing."

Jack and I talked for a few minutes and then he called our regular doctor in town, who also happens to be a good friend.

"It will be fine, Jack. I'll put you in touch with a breast surgeon first thing tomorrow morning."

The next morning, his nurse called. "I can get you an appointment at noon. It's in Bend. Would you like it?"

We took it, and in less than 24 hours after I first found out about the cancer, I was sitting in the surgeon's office, talking to him about it. We had a couple of alternatives: I could have a lumpectomy where they just remove that part of the breast where the actual cancer is, or a mastectomy where they remove the entire breast. The doctor gave me the statistics and a breast specialist, a woman, came in to help me with anything I might be struggling with. She gave me a box to take home that contained a video, a packet of information, some little chocolates and a journal to keep if I wanted to do that.

At home that evening, I watched the video. It was about women who had gone through breast cancer. They were talking about their choices and how they managed with their families or, as in some cases, without. The video bothered me because it seemed to be so focused on survival. The message that came through to me was, "You have to survive! Think positively and survive!" There was a small portion at the end that said, "And if a friend of yours doesn't..."

After I had watched the video, Jack joined me in the family room. He knelt before me and laid his head in my lap. As I gently ran my fingers through his thick, graying hair, we shared a moment where our two heartbeats became one.

"Let's have some coffee." He gently removed himself from my grasp and went to the kitchen. He padded back into the family room, barefoot, carefully carrying two hot mugs full to the brim with the delicious, nutty brew. He handed me a mug. I blew on the surface and then took a sip. Jack sat down beside me.

"Remember how, as young parents, we went to church 'just because?'"

Jack laughed. "Yeah. You just loved to dress the girls up in pretty dresses, hats and gloves."

Sighing, I said, "Yes, I was raised as a Catholic and I wanted the girls to go to church, but I didn't have a clue, honey. I had always understood what Jesus did for me, but I never knew anything about a personal relationship with the Lord."

"Well, at least you saw the inside of a church. I didn't have any religious upbringing at all. If you recall, when we went as a family, I was just along for the ride."

"When we changed churches and when we went to that marriage encounter in 1985, I had no idea what huge things in our lives they would be. That's when we learned that God is a real part of our lives, not a religious part."

"Patty, do you remember the question you asked me at that encounter?"

"Oh, sure. I asked you what would cause you to really believe that Jesus is who He says He is."

"And I said, 'I guess I would have to be struck like Paul.' And I was!"

"I'll never forget walking into our room at the encounter and finding you on the bed in tears, Jack."

"Yes," he said softly. "Sitting there on the bed, I said, 'God, if You are really, really here, You have to show me.' And then a presence came over me. It was like a flash of His voice in my soul, and I collapsed into tears."

Still thinking about the video, I said, "How any woman gets through something like this without God is a mystery to me."

The day of the surgery arrived. Jack was at the hospital with me and so was our oldest girl, Minta. I had opted for the lumpectomy so this was going to be an outpatient surgery. The doctor spent a lot of time talking with us, which was great because I had lots of questions. Then, as a courtesy, he left us alone for a few minutes and we prayed together.

As they were prepping me for surgery, a nurse took my blood pressure.

She looked at me with one eyebrow cocked. "117/60?"

"I'm truly not afraid of this. This is just part of life."

There were several weeks of healing after the lumpectomy. In the meantime, I went to the oncologist. He read the results of the breast tissue and the report on the five lymph nodes they had removed from under my arm.

They did this to see if any cancer had escaped into the lymph nodes.

Since everyone involved had said the cancer was caught early and was well contained, I was not expecting to have to do chemotherapy. However, I was supposed to have radiation for six weeks, five days a week, and I had to go to Bend for that. If I had had a mastectomy, they wouldn't have done any radiation.

"It's only six weeks and it's summer now so there won't be any trouble with the roads. It's not that big a deal."

The oncologist told me, "Everything is clear and looks good, but in the very last test they did on one lymph node, they found an active, fast-growing cancer cell. A year ago, we didn't have this test and we wouldn't have known it was there. It's contained, but since it's in a lymph node, we are going to have to do chemo."

"Oh, my gosh. Are you kidding?"

"Patty, that's how cancer travels through the body."

That was a disappointment to me. I had never given it a thought because this was an early detection.

The impressive thing about treatment is that everything is very individually set up. The drugs, the dosages, your hormones and the surgery all determine the kind of radiation and chemotherapy you will have. They take the time to set up an individual plan for every woman. I found that reassuring. Most people have eight sessions of chemotherapy. The oncologist said, "I think you will be fine with four, Patty."

Driving home after getting all the information from the oncologist, I had a question for my husband.

"Jack, what do you think will be the worst part of

chemotherapy?"

"Honey, you're going to lose your hair." There was a slight pause, and then he asked, "What do you think?"

"Throwing up! That will really be the worst thing for me." All my life, I had hated throwing up. It was the worst thing I could think of.

In June, I started chemo. As I was sitting on a chair in the room, the nurse put a plastic sheet under my arm.

"What's that for?"

"It's to protect the chair. If any of this gets on the chair, it will eat it away. It does some really damaging stuff. It kills a lot in the body."

I didn't think the nurse was supposed to tell me that.

"How remarkable that our veins can handle that! It says in the Bible that we are fearfully and wonderfully made."

She gave me a surprised look, but didn't comment further.

My hair started falling out on July 4th. It was very windy, and standing in the backyard, I noticed strands of hair blowing around in the air. I thought that was funny!

"Let's see what happens when I run my fingers through my hair." As I did that, it really started to come out in little bits all over the place.

Next, I decided to take a shower and wash my hair to see how much would come out. While I was in the shower, clumps of hair fell out and settled all over my body. My hair was pretty thick and quite a bit came out, but it was even and not patchy. The thought occurred to me to save some so I could compare the color from before the loss to the color afterward. I collected some and put it in a little bag.

Somehow, I was taking all of this like a little child.

"This is so interesting! Oh, wow! Look at this!" It was a huge new experience.

I didn't feel morbidly sick, and I didn't lose weight. It was weird, but as long as I kept eating during chemotherapy, I didn't lose weight. I even gained some! Also, I didn't throw up as much if I kept eating.

On a sunny, bright summer day, I thought, *You know, I am really tired of this hair.*

Calling my hairdresser, I was told she had an opening the next day. When I went for my appointment, she cut my hair very short. I recalled reading some of the literature I had been given, and I knew they recommended that you have it short because then you don't notice the fallout as much.

Jana was cutting and crying, and I said, "Really, Jana, it's okay."

She styled it in this little, short haircut, and the very next day, it totally fell out! That was the end of that.

It was time for wig research. On a trip to Bend, I decided to buy one. I went to some shops, tried some on and finally decided on a wig for cancer patients. It has a soft interior so it doesn't rub on your head.

"Let me see. Let's find one in a color that matches what my hair was when I was 20 years old." I had a chignon from back then so I picked out a wig in that color.

"My goodness! I feel like I am 20 again!" It was a cute little "do."

People commented. "Oh, I like your hair."

One day a pastor in town said, "I really like your hair!"

"It's not my hair. I'm a cancer patient and it's a wig."

He was horrified, but it became a great joke. It got

to where he would say, "I really like your hair," and I would respond, "If you want to borrow it, you can. When I am finished with it, I'll give it to you."

Another discovery — without hair, your head gets very cool! It was summer and I was grateful. Often, I would go around the house without wearing the wig because I would get tired of it. A few times I answered the door, forgot I wasn't wearing it, and shocked some people.

Going out in public was a different story. Some people are comfortable not wearing a wig, but I felt going out without it would draw attention to myself in a way that I didn't care to do.

One day, Jack came home early from work and I wasn't wearing my wig.

"Do you see what a cute, little, round head I have?"

He came up behind me, put his arms around me and pulled me back against him. "It's the cutest little, round head I've ever seen!" He kissed me right on top.

By Thanksgiving, I had a little hair growing back. I had just finished chemotherapy the end of September, but by Thanksgiving, I had a head of very short hair. We had Thanksgiving dinner with Jack's family in Portland and I didn't wear my wig. My hair was very short and I have kept it short. The texture has changed so I am having fun experimenting with my hair.

Chemotherapy was very hard. I threw up a lot and I tried to remember to keep eating. It wasn't like throwing up when you are sick with the flu. It would come upon me suddenly, with no warning, and many times, I just barely made it to the bathroom.

I sat around a lot because chemo makes you very tired. Because my immune system was way down, the doctor told me not to be around people. It was just too risky. The chemo drugs are working to kill things in your body.

There was one thing I had to do. I just had to go to church. "Lord, I need to be there. I need to praise and worship You, so will You protect me in terms of who's around me?"

I asked God for protection to go to church, not for any legalistic reason, but because of my relationship with Him. He gave me that protection.

It was summer so there weren't a lot of colds and things going around. That was good, but I still had to avoid gatherings. Jack's aunt died of breast cancer during this time, but I couldn't go to the funeral because there were too many people. The doctor said, "I don't think it's a wise thing to do."

For my radiation treatments, I had to go to Bend every day except Saturday and Sunday. They tattooed my chest because they have to put the radiation in exactly the same spot every time. There was this thick foam pillow where you have your arms up and your head lays down into it. The stuff hardens and conforms to your shape. You lay down in that pillow every time, and the rays from the radiation machine go into the same spot on your body every time. The treatments last three minutes at the most.

I was warned to use the creams they gave me. Toward the end, there was some redness and soreness, like a sunburn, but it was only in the last week.

All the people who dealt with me were wonderful. They were compassionate. They wanted to take care of me. The doctors explained things thoroughly. They made me a part of the whole process and it really helped.

After the radiation, I began to take a drug called Tamoxifen, but I just couldn't tolerate it. They had two Aromatace inhibitors. The side effects were too much for me. Huge bruises developed on my legs. They stayed red and didn't turn black and blue. It was supposed to be a long-term follow-up treatment.

The oncologist suggested that we try Herceptin. This is a relatively new drug, an IV drip. It has to be given within two years of your original diagnosis. You also have to meet certain other criteria in order to take it, and if you do, it is supposed to be very good for prevention. He said, "Let's do that."

I had to go into the chemotherapy room for my treatments every three weeks for a year. Going back into the chemo room again, with its familiar smell, and being around people who are very sick, some even close to death, was very difficult. I had to remind myself that I was totally in God's hands.

My veins seem to be almost worn out. They can't use the arm where the breast cancer was so they always used the other one. Over the course of this past year, it has become more difficult to get a needle into the veins. A couple of times I have fainted because once they get the needle in, they start moving it around. Jack tells them, "She'll be okay."

He holds me while they go get a washcloth or put my head down until I come around. "Oops. Sorry."

The follow-up goes on for a long time. They check me frequently and carefully. There is no such thing as "regular" mammograms for me anymore. They have me come back for more mammograms and ultrasounds at the slightest hint of a problem. They will even insert a needle and extract fluid to be sure it's just a cyst. They are constantly watching to see if anything is developing again.

I schedule my mammograms for when the radiologist is there and he can talk to me. Last spring, when I went in and had a mammogram, he said, "I don't think there's anything to worry about. It looks clear to me." They decided to put it through some other kind of computer to read, also.

We were on our way to visit our daughter, Leila, who lives in Arkansas. I had mammograms on Friday, and we left the following Monday with a truck because we were taking her some furniture. We were clear across the country, in the middle of nowhere, and as soon as we approached a little town, my cell phone rang and there was a message waiting. "Well, there seems to be some question about that last mammogram."

We expected to be in Arkansas for three weeks with our daughter. I called them and said, "I can't get back."

"We don't think it's anything urgent. Don't worry about it. We will schedule you just as soon as you get back."

Sitting quietly in the truck, I thought, "Oh, no. Is this going to start all over again?" Shifting in my seat, I turned to look at my husband.

"Jack, I am not doing this over. If there is anything wrong, I will have a double mastectomy. I don't care. I'm cutting these things off!"

"Okay, honey. I know. I understand."

That was discouraging. After all I had been through, I wasn't able to think about going through it again.

I don't even know if they would have let me go through radiation and chemo again. I don't know what the choices would have been. All I knew was that I was in Arkansas for three weeks, and I had all that time to think about it.

"Lord, I am going to trust You. But I don't understand this. Have I not trusted You enough?"

We had a wonderful time with Leila and her husband, Travis. They have an old Victorian house and we helped them paint, do some repairs and run errands. But this mammogram question was in the back of my mind the whole time.

When we returned, I had to go through several procedures. By the time Sunday rolled around, the test results still weren't very clear yet. At our church, we have a time before the service where we have praise and prayer. Some people stand around the edges of the church, making themselves available to pray for others, and if you need prayer, you can go to them. I had made up my mind that I was going to ask for prayer and confirmation of a healing. Just as I was ready to approach someone, the woman who was the head of the prayer team came up to me and said, "Would you mind praying for people today? Carla is home sick and we need someone to take her place."

"I would be happy to do that. As a matter of fact, I was going to ask prayer myself."

"Let's pray for you right now." She called another woman over to join us.

"I just had some follow-up mammograms and there are some questions. I just want to agree that nothing is wrong." We prayed together.

It was a real blessing for me to be able to pray for some other people that morning. "God, it is such grace that You did this for me. You are so amazing."

From Panic to Peace

When I went back for the second mammogram, they said, "We don't know why, but now we are not seeing anything in that area."

Well, I believed God had removed it.

It was crazy for a while because they kept questioning whether or not it was there. We went back and forth. "Okay, God's done it." "No." "Yes."

They were being so careful, looking for a little something that they had previously seen.

"I trust God in this." That was the bottom line for me.

God had groomed me, prepared me and put me in a very protected place in His hand before I even knew what was going on. I knew that my attitude was the only thing that showed how much I trusted God.

My hope is that December will be the end of this laborious process for me, the end of treatment. No doubt, I will have to see the oncologist for a long time.

The only time I felt depressed was right after viewing that video I had been given. I was so sorry for those women because survival was their only hope. I thought, *My hope isn't in survival. It's in Jesus Christ and the promises of God. I'll survive in the way God wants me to. That's the only important thing to me. Whether it's here or in heaven. As Paul, the apostle, said, "To die is Christ." I would like to live for my family and friends, but if I die, I will be with Christ and that's even better!*

The night I watched the video, I didn't sleep well. I just wanted to reach out and touch those women, all the women going through this experience, and share God with them and the privilege of being able to walk so closely with Him through something this difficult. I want to reach all women with that message. If you really know God, you won't be so concerned about how things will turn out because God's in control.

Sarah's Story
as told by Maryl Smith

Our faded green Packard rumbled as we wound down the old gravel country road and headed deeper out into the timber and bushes. The crunchy sounds faded as the roadbed changed from gravel to dirt and then eventually stopped when there was no more road. I stared out the window as the dust swirled and then settled down in this remote grassy field. *Here it comes*, a voice roared in my head. The roaring grew until everything outside the car faded into sepia tones, and I fled the external world to escape down the tunnel in my mind. Feelings shrank away and I became a small Sarah, monotone and unnoticeable. This small me climbed onto a tiny shelf in the back of my head and curled into a fetal position.

"Time to get out, Sarah. We're going to play the spanking game." My father's deep voice invaded the barrier and reverberated in my internal darkness. I was mercilessly sucked back through the dark tunnel and slammed into his reality. But I left my little Sarah behind on her shelf. She would have the sweet illusion of safety. My Sarah would remain innocent.

"Here, let me help you take your clothes off," he offered, and I obediently relented. I knew the routine. My grooming for this role had started when I was 3 years old. I watched, detached, as my dad's familiar sun-browned hands slowly undressed me and then fastened a belt around my wrists. These were the same hands that always hugged me when I made good grades or soothed me when I was sick. Now they pulled the leather strap so tight that my hands tingled. The dichotomy of his hands was lost on me at the time. It was just the way that life was.

Dad stretched my skinny frame over the hood of the

car and tied me face down. I could feel the radiance from the engine-warmed hood permeate my belly. A resounding snap and the searing sting of a leather strap slamming into my backside shattered the moment of warmth. The blows came one after another with increasing intensity. I shut all feelings down, except for the warmth that flowed from the car into my belly. I imagined that the distant belt, raising pink welts on my body, was a terrible self-mobilized entity, not an extension of my dad's wonderful hands. But the blows soon became more frenzied and the sting eventually found its way to my nerve endings. So did the sounds of raspy breathing from his exertion and arousal.

I broke into sobs. "Daddy, please stop. It hurts." The world stood still momentarily, and then his soothing voice penetrated my panic.

"It's going to be okay, Sarah. You'll like this. It helps me feel good when you do this for me."

After the sex was over, Dad put his arms around me and hugged me. "I love you, Sarah. You are a special little girl. Remember, this is our secret. No one else would understand. They might think that you are bad." His face had a funny look, a little bit like reassurance with a mixture of sorrow. On the ride home we didn't talk. I stared blankly out the window and began to daydream that I was somewhere else, outside the car running along in the brush... as free as a wild stallion.

Looking back, I will never completely understand why my dad, a good man in so many ways, was so ill. He was not the kind of guy you would ever expect to be an abuser. He was outgoing, friendly and well-known in community affairs, an all-around good guy. I do know that his problems began when he returned from serving overseas in World War II. He was in the 10th Armored Division. The Germans surrounded his unit in Bastogne, and the dwindling survivors fought for days with no food and little ammunition before help arrived. He lived through horrific events that he would never discuss. After the war, there were no veterans' services available to help soldiers process their experiences. They had to pretend like nothing had happened and were expected to resume life with the agony buried under a surface facade.

When Dad returned home from overseas, he was a totally different man than the one my mom had married. She wanted to leave him, but found out she was pregnant with me. I wasn't wanted and so Mom never felt a natural inclination to nurture me. I have no memories of my mother holding or rocking me. But Dad said that he wanted to have a baby because he wanted something good after the war. I was very special to him, so special that he became obsessed with me.

All of my childhood years were spent living with our extended family, including my grandpa and uncles. We were like a huge group of gypsies, traveling from place to place to follow the construction work. We lived in trailers, tarps and tents, clustered together in the woods. Everything was done together. There was closeness and a special bond in that kind of living that also had its secret, dark side. Dad was into Edgar Casey and the science of the mind, while Mom delved into potions, séances, pendulum readings, tarot cards, Ouija boards and incantations. I was born a day before Halloween, so Mom always said that I was a proper witch. Since we never stayed long enough anywhere to form friendships, the underbelly of our life was never exposed.

Sarah's Story

Our own 20-foot camp trailer had a hotplate, heater and a sink with only cold water. There was no bathroom and we had to use any nearby truck stop for our personal needs. Mom and Dad slept in the single bedroom in the back, and my older sister and I slept in the living space on the futon-style couch that was folded up during the day. When Mom would leave the trailer, Dad would say, "Come in here. I have something to show you," and lead me into the dark and musty back room. Sitting on the bed, he exposed himself and explained, "I want to talk to you about what this is. It is important to know that girls and boys are different and that there is nothing to be afraid of." At first, his talk was calming. I had no clue what was going on. The lessons moved from looking to touching. He wanted me to be comfortable with this, but I never was. Like any child, I just knew that it was important to always do what my father said. By the time I was 10 years old, it progressed to more than just touching. Rape became a pattern that lasted throughout all my young life, until I turned 18 and left home. Sometimes Dad would quote Bible stories to me about how Lot's daughters laid down with their father and had sex. He would explain that because it was in the Bible, it was okay. When you are young, you don't question those things, you just believe them. Dad would always say to me, "This is your little secret," as if it were something I wanted him to do. Sometimes he would warn me, "It would be cruel of you to say anything to anybody. If you do, I will have to spank you because this would just ruin your mother."

Various forms of abuse became an everyday event. He developed a hand signal, and when Mom was not looking, he would flash the signal. I was expected to expose myself to him. This kept me under the gun all the time so I never felt comfortable about bringing friends home to visit. Between the constant moving from place to place and the abuse at home, I was unable to develop any lasting friendships or find anyone trustworthy enough to tell.

By the time I was a teen, Dad would encourage me to be promiscuous with the boys I dated. When I returned home, I was expected to describe the salient details to him. I tried to pretend that nothing ever happened to avoid his interrogations. I never thought about actually not having sex. I figured that I was already dirty, so what difference did it make if I had sex with all these boys? Unable to get satisfactory details from me, my dad began to arrange dates for me with older men from his work. He would tell them that I would have sex with them and that he expected to get a report. This time, I got angry and refused to cooperate. He quit this tactic after awhile because it wasn't productive for him. It was the first time I discovered that I could have some control.

The downside of my new belligerence was that the episodes with my father progressed into forms of torture. We would take our journey, by car, to an abandoned shed where he would tie me up with a rope and hoist me, naked, off the ground by tossing the rope over the rafters. Then Dad would beat me with the belt, willow switches or anything that wouldn't show too much bruising on the outside. The whole time, he would verbally reassure me with soft and gentle words. The dichotomy of both violence and tenderness coming at me at the same time split me into two worlds. I longed for a knight in shining armor, but at the same time, I got the evil ogre. So I separated my true inner being from the violent dad. She stayed on the corner shelf in my mind all of the time and didn't know about the terrible events of life. I called her "MY Sarah." It was "THE Sarah" that suffered. She carried on with our outside life while my baby child remained protected from everything, waiting for a prince to come and awaken her.

I developed huge control issues. I was hyper vigilant about my environment and worked hard to try and keep safe. Dad pushed me into deception, lying to Mom and keeping secrets. THE Sarah became good at this, and Mom seemed completely oblivious of everything that was happening. Meanwhile, I indulged in high-risk behavior. My idea of fun was destroying graveyards or attempting to blow up the back of the local jail with dynamite.

Then, one amazing day, I met Tom. Could a man like this be real? There wasn't any deception or meanness to him at all. When I was with him, I felt like the most beautiful and good person in the world. Somehow, I knew I was completely safe in his arms and my heart dared to love someone. We became engaged. Then my hyper vigilance kicked back into gear and doubts began to run rampant through my head. *Am I just using him to get away from home? Is this really love? How do I know what love is? Does he deserve to be stuck with someone like me?* I decided to take one month off from our relationship until I knew for sure. My parents were overjoyed at the breakup. They thought that it was a done deal.

In the month that followed, I realized that I wasn't just using Tom as an escape. I really did love this man for who he was. I loved who I was when I was with him, so I joyfully renewed our relationship. My parents were furious. They couldn't control me any longer. "You are too young and too stupid for marriage," my mom hissed, as she pulled a battered suitcase out of the closet and began to throw my clothes into a jumbled heap. "How could you be so ungrateful?" She slammed the lid down with finality and stormed out of the room.

Dad only offered stony silence as he tossed my suitcase into his car and drove me to a motel. When we arrived, he handed me a $100 bill, bid me a hasty, "Goodbye and don't ever come back," and then drove away, leaving me standing alone on the curb.

Tom's mom graciously allowed me to move in with her until the wedding. My parents steadfastly refused to help, but did permit me to use their name on the invitation. When I went back home later to pick up the rest of my things, there was nothing to collect. My mom had thrown everything out. Upon my request, Dad showed up at the ceremony to give me away, but never spoke to me throughout the entire event. It hurt, but I was happy. I had Tom.

One drizzly day, I was cleaning house and heard an unexpected knock at my door while Tom was at work. I opened the door to find my dad's muscular frame leaning against the doorpost. He had a kind and empathetic look on his face. "May I come in?" he gently asked. I looked up at the gentlemanly face that I knew so well. I still desperately wanted him to be my hero; every little girl wants that from her dad. Hope welled up within me that he had come to reconcile. I let him in and happily prepared two cups of coffee for our reunion. However, it quickly became clear that he had come to the house with other intentions. He wanted sex, and before I knew it, our reconciliation collapsed into a nightmare. His visit quickly ended with me yelling at him to stay away from me and kicking him out the door.

That night, when Tom came home from work, he met me in the hallway. Oblivious to the day's events, he put his arms around me and leaned down to give me a kiss. I went ballistic! I began to scream and beat him on the chest. Then I sunk to the floor in tears, sobbing. Tom was stunned and completely bewildered about what had just happened. He sat down beside me on the floor and gingerly asked, "What in the world is going on?" For the first time in my life, it all spilled out: what Dad had done to me in the past and what he had tried to do to me today. I felt embarrassed and completely afraid of how my husband would react. Tom was livid. As soon as he had gained better control over his emotions, he drove straight to Dad's house and took him out for a cup of coffee. It wasn't one of those friendly coffee klatch conversations. Tom threatened, "If you ever even hint about touching Sarah again, I will literally have your head. You are never to approach her or touch her again." With that ominous warning, it seemed like the nightmare of my childhood was finally over. Tom became the knight in shining armor I had always longed for. After that event, we maintained only a carefully limited relationship with my folks. I certainly never let my children be around Dad without supervision at all times.

I thought that my past was behind me and that it couldn't hurt me anymore. But it left me with problems that I didn't even recognize at the time. I never cried or expressed emotion. I had been trained too well all of my life to keep the feelings stuffed down and hidden. I continued to use the hyper vigilance that had helped me to survive as a youth, only now it didn't seem to serve me. It is very mentally tiring to try to anticipate everything others will do or say. It makes it hard to just experience and enjoy life as it unfolds. I developed real problems with sex in our marriage. It became so difficult to cope with my feelings and reactions that I eventually lost all interest.

When the younger of my two daughters turned 5, we brought a teenage girl into our house to live with us to protect her from abuse at home by her brothers. My heart just broke for her, and I was trying to work with her to open up about the abuse in her life. There was only one problem with that: I hadn't really dealt with my own abuse yet. I began to suffer horrendous migraine headaches. The doctor ran several tests, but couldn't find anything wrong. Despite the fact we couldn't find a physical cause, I required two hospitalizations to medicate the pain. One day, my pain was so bad that I passed out in our hallway. Once again, Tom took me to the hospital, and while I was there, it all became too much for me to handle. I went into a catatonic state and completely shut down. I could hear and feel everything from a distance, but I couldn't move or respond. I remember laying there while the doctor slapped my face and stuck needles in my feet, trying to get a reaction from me. Inside I was crying because I couldn't respond even though it hurt. I was slammed back in time to when my dad had poked me with pins in my private parts. As the doctor yelled at me and popped off obscenities at my lack of response, I fell into deeper internal turmoil. Memories of my abuse came flooding back like virtual reality. Then, in the midst of the chaos, an amazing thing happened. As I was sliding down, down into that terrible black hole, I sensed that God had taken hold of me. I could feel His hand underneath me and His gentle reassurance. I felt Him say, *It's going to be okay.*

Tom had been gone when this event was happening. When he came back, I was finally able to break out of my stupor and started to cry, rocking back and forth to self-comfort. I reverted to a time when I thought I had been safe and became a 5-year-old child. So there I sat, hugging a toilet paper roll like a cherished teddy bear, sobbing and calling for my mommy. For some reason, that roll of toilet paper seemed like my only point of security in the whole world. Nothing else was safe. The nurses couldn't get me to relinquish the toilet paper for anything. So they did the next logical thing. I was admitted into the psychiatric ward.

I was an inpatient for six weeks and, in all of that time, there was no real progress. The ward was mostly for warehousing while medication levels were adjusted. During my first session with a psychiatrist, I disclosed the long-lived abuse with my father. "Well, you must have enjoyed it," was his only comment.

The psychologist took a different tactic by using role play, and it was in this session that I had my awakening. He was Dad and I, the child, was to tell him where I was emotionally hurting. He sat in that chair across the sparse room and continued to prod me with comments until I suddenly became angry. "You didn't protect me!" I blurted out. "I never felt that you took care of me. Why did you hurt me like that? Dads are supposed to love their children!" I bolted out of my chair and began to pace the room, aching to rip apart something or pound on the walls. The words came like rapid fire. "You took away my virginity. You ruined my sex life with my husband." I took a final shuddering breath and fell in a heap to the floor. "Dad, you took away my entire childhood!" I completely spent myself in the rage, and when I came back to myself, I was shocked. I hadn't had a clue how angry I was. The experience was a big steam release for me, and suddenly I knew I had some unfinished work to do to heal all of that pain.

Meanwhile, an acquaintance from work loaned me a book to read while I was in the hospital. She was a lively woman named Jean. Despite the hectic pace of the workplace, I had noticed that she carried herself with a peace, joy and comfort with life that I didn't have. The book she loaned me was *The Cross and the Switchblade*, a story about a gang leader named Nicky Cruz. Nicky experienced the love of Jesus and was healed from his addiction and violent lifestyle. I devoured the entire book while I was there, and then shared it with Tom. The story struck a chord in my heart. Maybe God could change my messed up life, too. I longed to believe that. I wondered about my experience in the emergency room. Had God really talked to me? Did He really want to take care of me?

I began outpatient sessions to deal with the reality of my abuse and to learn how I had turned my anger into unhealthy behavior. It was good to finally tell the secret, but reliving the events was nightmarish. At least this time, I didn't have to go through the abuse all alone.

After a few months in therapy, our insurance man invited me to church. It was an interesting experience. There was something different there. I could feel the presence of God, but I didn't know how to respond to it. Then a new movie came to town. It was based upon the Nicky Cruz book that I had read in the hospital. Jean invited Tom and me to go, and we planned a double date with her and her boyfriend, Jack.

When Jean introduced us to Jack, Tom's mouth dropped open in disbelief. Jean's boyfriend also happened to be Tom's old bosom buddy from childhood. Jack had gone to Vietnam and came back bitter. When he dove into drugs for solace, he and Tom no longer had anything in common. They had parted ways. Now here he was, healthy, vibrant and happy. Tom was mesmerized by the change. After the movie, we went out for pizza. Over pepperoni and double cheese, Tom asked Jack, "What happened, man? You were a dedicated stoner."

Jack smiled. "God saved my weary behind, and I didn't need the drugs anymore. I used to drown out my experiences from 'Nam. Jesus healed my anger and bitterness. I don't need to numb my feelings anymore." Tom was impressed, but that's about as far as it went at the time.

Meanwhile, I continued to process my abuse with a loving therapist and a group of other women who had experienced similar pain. We walked through everything together from the feelings of isolation to a lifelong sense that we were dirty, all the way through the pain and grief of not having a father's protection. We each grieved our losses, our childhoods, and the fact that our fathers and mothers weren't saviors. Walking through my life again, pulling it apart and then learning to put it all back together with a healthy perspective was so important. But, at times, it got downright scary. Thank heaven God gave me an amazing gift in my husband. Tom was the most understanding, helpful person. Sometimes he didn't even know if he was going to have a wife left during the dark season of my healing process, but he never left my side.

There was also a positive side to the review of my life; I got to relive the good things in my childhood, too. I was able to take MY Sarah off the hidden shelf and re-experience the better moments with her. My inner child was coming out and feeling safe. She learned to receive emotional nourishment from my adult self and from other people around her. These moments satisfied the deep deprivation left by our mother. Sometimes I would go to the store for bread and milk and come back with ice cream or rag dolls instead. Before the process was complete, I had bought 50 rag dolls. Tom tolerated it all with good humor, although our bedroom was getting mighty crowded. So I settled on a favorite and named her "My Mary." She went to bed with me every night.

Somewhere in the middle of my therapy, Nicky Cruz came to town and Tom and I went to hear him speak. At the end of his talk, he invited people who wanted to begin a life with Jesus to come down to the front to pray. Tom and I were both standing there with tears rolling down our cheeks. We had seen the truth of what that could mean in our lives. We saw it in Jean and in Jack. With everything inside of me, I wanted to go forward and pray, but not without Tom. So we simply turned around and left. It was like standing in front of this huge banquet table filled with the most succulent, mouth-watering food in the whole world and then turning your back and walking away starving.

Two weeks later, I was still unsatisfied and hungry for something, so I went to church with a friend. That Sunday, there was a missionary speaker who shared story after story about how Jesus was changing lives

Sarah's Story

within the gypsy community in France. It struck so close
to home. Each one of those stories could have been me
or members of my family! Then he invited people to
come forward for an altar call. I didn't know what that
was, but people were going up to a little rail with
benches and kneeling at the front of the church, so I
went, too. I knelt and started to pray. Suddenly, I felt
overwhelming guilt for living my life without God. I
knew that I wanted to know Jesus personally. So I told
Him that I was sorry, and I asked Him to help me. Then
the most amazing thing happened. I felt the love and acceptance of God pour over me, and I began to cry and
pray without reservation. I knew that I was loved, and
there was nothing that I had ever done to deserve it. I
have never doubted His love ever since that experience.
Later, I talked to the pastor and asked him what had happened to me. He suggested that I could learn more about
it in the Bible from stories about others who had the
same experience. He recommended the book of Ro-
mans, chapter 3:23-25 and chapter 10:8-11.

Late that evening, after the swing shift, when Tom
walked through the door, he found me in a halo of lamp-
light, sitting at the kitchen table, voraciously reading.
Later he told me, "I thought something was terribly
wrong because you were reading the Bible and we just
don't do that. You had this weird glow about you, and I
wasn't sure that it was completely from the lamp."

When Tom asked what was going on, I paused for a
moment and then replied, "I don't know how to tell you
what I experienced. You need to come with me tomorrow morning to church and see for yourself."

He reacted with a defensive "humph," followed by a
cursory, "No." The next day, he silently got dressed and

went to church. The same speaker was there. Tom does-n't remember to this day what that guy said. All that he remembers is that he ran up for the altar call and stood there for half an hour, crying and opening his heart to the healing love of God.

We were both changing so much. Over all, it took me about four years to work through the problems and grief that the abuse had brought into my life. There were a lot of emotional ups and downs in the process, but I am so glad that Jesus and Tom both walked with me on that journey. I gradually learned to cherish times of intimacy with my husband without the past intruding, and that has been such a precious gift. Now I have the ability to be a whole person, my child self and my adult self at the same time. I have learned to feel and to ex-press my emotions. Man, it hurt to learn how to express the pain! But the process worked just like using the pull cord on a two-sided curtain. When I pulled back the covering on the negative emotions, the curtain on the other side opened, too. Gradually, I learned to play and to feel joy and wonder again. I felt like Dorothy in *The Wizard of Oz*, stepping out of the sepia tones of Kansas and into a world of color with sights and sounds of pure enjoyment.

The therapy helped me with everyday living, but it didn't cover my most important spiritual need. One day in church, our pastor gave a sermon about not forgiving and how it can control our hearts and destroy our experi-ence of life. Even though I still had some relationship with Dad, I had never actually forgiven him. The ser-mon seemed unfair. I couldn't imagine that God ex-pected me to forgive Dad, and I wondered what forgiv-ing him would mean. Were forgiveness and trust the same thing? Did it mean that Dad got off the hook scot-free? I needed to understand, and so I went up to the altar at the front of the church and knelt down to pray. "Jesus, how do I do this? I don't have the ability to forgive him, but I want to learn. I need Your help. I am ready to go on a forgiveness exploration with You, but You are going to have to lead the way. I don't even know where the trail begins."

And so, God began to take me on the path to forgiveness. The first step of our journey began in the same place that all spiritual life seems to begin, in Jesus' suffering and death upon the cross. I already knew that, in that act, He took upon himself any punishment that I deserved for hurting others. Now, as I read about the atrocities that He endured at the time of His death, I found myself relating to His pain. Suddenly, the reverse relationship dawned upon me; Jesus understood! He knew every feeling that I went through during my abuse because He has been there. He was an innocent person, yet He endured humiliation and the feeling of being totally alone during His abuse. He never said a word. He took the beatings and stood stark naked in front of people, even in front of His own mother. As He looked down upon His abusers from the cross, He knew firsthand how deeply we can hurt one another by our sin. In that moment, He not only offered to take the pain of that sin upon Himself, but He also took upon Himself all of the grief and sorrow thrust upon us by the sin of others. He took responsibility for every form of pain that drives people to hurt one another in their ignorance. In deep compassion, He cried out for all of us, "Father, forgive them because they don't understand what they are doing."

I was stunned. I knew that I had no other choice but to do the same thing that He had done. I needed to forgive my dad. I wanted that depth of love to be not only in my own life, but to reach my dad as well. After that, I prayed every day for an entire month that Jesus would help me to forgive my dad. Then, one day, the need to pray that prayer was gone. A huge weight lifted off of me and the heaviness and anger was gone. It had melted away, bit by bit, as I prayed each day. The change in me was dramatic. I felt alive! It was like a resurrection! Only by experiencing it myself could I have ever understood the miracle of forgiveness. I learned that the resentment festering in my heart had fermented and mutated into the ugly form of bitterness. I had grown into an angry person, and that anger had been chewing away at me and destroying me from the inside out. My refusal to forgive didn't hurt Dad; it had hurt me! The day I chose to forgive Dad, I didn't take a key and just let him out of prison for the wrongs he had done. Instead, I had let myself out of a prison and then turned around and handed the key to Jesus. God could decide what to do with Dad, whether that meant forgiveness or whether that meant punishment. I was no longer in control of the matter. I can't begin to tell you how that lesson has helped me. After that, I kept praying for my parents, but did not see any change throughout the many years that followed.

One day, I read an interesting verse in the Bible. It seemed to say that prayer could demolish any warped thinking or evil barriers in people's minds that prevent them from being able to experience the love of God. Somewhat incredulous, I went to my pastor and said, "I just read 2 Corinthians 10:4-5. Can my prayers really tear down strongholds and evil influences that affect other people's minds? Can we actually do that for other people?"

A big grin spread all over his face, like a kid who had just been given a big bag of candy. "Sure, why not?" he responded. I was elated.

After that conversation, Tom and I went camping in the Ochocos in the middle of August. I decided not to eat one meal each day and use that time to pray for my folks in this way. I was having so much fun with this method that I soon cut out a second meal to pray. By the end of the trip, I was totally fasting and praying for my parents at every mealtime. All in all, we spent three weeks there, digging for thunder eggs and praying.

The next Christmas, my parents came to visit, and for the first time, they attended church with us. It was a lovely candlelight service and when they arrived at our home afterwards, I noticed a distinct difference in them. We all sat down for some spiced holiday tea and contentment radiated from them and warmed the entire room. Finally, I had to say something about it. "There's something different about you two. I need to know what that is. What has happened?" At first they waved me off, but I persisted. "No, there really is something different."

Dad and Mom gave each other a glance that seemed to say, "we're busted!" Then Dad sheepishly said, "Well, I guess we better tell you." He took another long sip from his tea to let the tension build. "Last summer, your mom and I were reading in our Bible and realized we were attending church, but didn't really know the Jesus that the Bible was talking about. So we talked about it and then knelt by the bed. We both asked Him to come into our lives. He did. Now that we know Him, we have decided that we want to serve Him."

I had been holding my breath in suspense. The question burst out of me like an explosion. "Dad, when did this happen?"

Dad thoughtfully ran his fingers through his salt and pepper hair, and then fixed me with those deep, black eyes. "Oh, about the third week of August." That was the same time that I had fasted and prayed for them! God had answered my prayers right away and I never knew it until now. We talked for a long time that night and found that they had not only changed, but had stopped doing all the other weird spiritual stuff. When Jesus heals a broken family, He doesn't mess around. I was ecstatic with happiness.

Every one of us has changed. Now I can talk about what happened to me without cringing. I grew into so much freedom that one year, I decided that I needed to tell my mom about the abuse. I wanted our family to be free from secrets. Tom took Dad out and warned him that she was going to be told, while I sat down with my mom and explained what had happened to me as a child. Her only response was, "Well, that doesn't surprise me. Your dad was taught in college that the right thing to do is to teach your children about sex." When Tom and Dad got back, we all talked about it together. We each agreed that God had forgiven us and so we forgave each other. We wanted the truth in the open so that we were free to love each other. At the end of the evening, we prayed together and asked God to heal the whole thing and put it in the past. I thought that it was done, but one week later, I got a letter from my mother. She accused me of being mean, cruel and vindictive to bring this up after all of these years. Normally, my response to this kind of letter wouldn't have been very good. This time I understood that she had her own hurt that needed time to heal. I never responded to Mom's letter with anything except prayer. Once she got past her hurt and anger, we developed a close bond. Only one thing remained to be done.

I sincerely wanted to personally tell my dad that I had forgiven him. I asked Jesus for the perfect opportunity. It happened at my parents' 50th wedding anniversary. My sister and I put together a big party in the VFW hall. We hired a band, decorated the whole place with yellow streamers and had a white cake reception table. There were toasts and dancing all evening; Mom and Dad loved to dance. We attached big metal washers onto the strings of dozens of yellow helium balloons. When air moved in the room, the balloons would waltz about the floor.

Then the miracle moment came. Dad walked up to me and bowed. "May I have the honor of this dance?" I nodded and stepped within his arms and he proceeded to sweep me across the floor. After a minute, Dad began to speak so softly that it was hard to hear him over the thrumming of the music. "Honey, I don't know how to ask you this thing." He paused, obvious emotion welling up in his eyes. "I know I hurt you very badly when you were a child. I was wrong. I don't deserve anything, but will you forgive me?"

I looked into his troubled eyes and smiled. "Dad, I have already forgiven you. I forgave you years ago." Now, both of us had teary eyes as he swirled me gently around the floor. It was a dream-like moment, suspended in time amidst the floating clouds of shiny, yel-

low balloons. They spun around us like enchanted danc-
ers as my dad and I experienced the miracle of grace. I
became his little girl and he was finally my knight in
shining armor, just like a kingdom fairytale. We stayed
on the dance floor until the tears disappeared, but that
moment will never leave me.

Since then, Dad has asked me many times to forgive
him. It seems that he can never quite believe that the
miracle is true. Mother passed away a couple of years
ago. I was able to be with her, read scriptures to her and
pray during her passing. It was a very special time between me, my mom and the Lord. To this day, I am still
close to my dad. I know how rare it is for reconciliation
to happen between people when this type of thing has
happened. In most cases, an ongoing relationship isn't
possible or even recommended. Only the transforming
love of Jesus coming to each of us, bringing the gift of
forgiveness and healing, could make us a family again.
When I visit Dad in assisted living, we spend our time
talking about what we read in the Bible and what God is
showing us.

Some people ask, "Why would God allow you to go
through all that stuff? What kind of sadistic God do you
have?" God doesn't make choices to hurt others. People
do. As for the arduous process of healing, why should I
regret the wonderful things He has taught me through
suffering? I wouldn't trade what I have learned on the
path of healing for anything. Jesus has helped me to become a better person instead of a bitter one. I have
come out of the long, dark tunnel of abuse to the other
side, rich with wisdom, knowledge and depth of character. I am able to help other people who have been hurt,

and that is no small joy. I have the gift of my church. God made churches so that we will never be alone in our pain and we can learn to grow into a healthy, loving family.

I am an overcomer. My story lies here on the pages of this book because I know there are others who are hurting like I was. If you are one of them, I invite you to join me on the tumultuous and miraculous journey to healing. Jesus will be our tour guide, and believe me, from one risk taker to another, it'll be the ride of your life!

A Shattered Life Restored

Will Robbins' story
as told by Peggy Thompson

"There he is! My idol!"

Shrinking back behind the corner of the cafeteria, I flattened myself against the cement wall. There was this tremendous urge to poke my head out a little so I could watch him. Jerry was "royalty," the coolest guy at Sacramento High School.

My heart hammered against my chest as I furtively watched him swagger along the cement walk. He wore the *cool* blue jeans, a plaid shirt and construction-type work boots. His hair was long. It was the *only* way to dress. He was everything I wanted to be. Confidence just oozed from his person and I could feel it where I stood, a good 75 feet away. In contrast, I was a too-tall kid, I was fat and I had a face full of pimples. The school bullies often laid in wait for me. They would knock me around and steal my lunch money. But I knew they wouldn't dare challenge Jerry. Breathing a sigh of relief, I relaxed as he turned toward a path that was going off in another direction. He wasn't going to pass by me, after all. Starting to walk away in the opposite direction, hands jammed into my pockets and my head drooping, I realized how much I hated myself. There wasn't anything cool about me.

"Hey, Will! Over here!"

Someone was yelling at me from the rear of a portable classroom. Turning in that direction, I recalled that some of us were going to smoke cigarettes back there during lunch.

"Did you forget?" Ben asked as I approached.

"No, I didn't forget."

"What are you so grouchy about?"

"Nothin'. Come on. Let's go."

We gathered behind the building. It was a hot September day in Sacramento, but there was a hint of fall in the air. The wind was softly sighing through the trees that lined the rear of the building. The leaves were starting to fall and colors were starting to turn.

There was a small pile of them on the ground in hues of gold and red, and I tromped on them, listening to the crunch.

We stood around smoking, feeling bold and adventurous, when I became aware that some of the guys had started poking fun at me. This was not a new experience for me, but my friends usually accepted me as one of their own. On this day, things would change. There was a feeling in the air, like I was standing on the brink of some new but nameless experience. The sound of Carl's voice brought me back to the moment.

"Hey, Will, how come your mom and dad never come to parent conferences or anything?"

I threw a nervous glance in the direction of my best friend, Ben.

"Will doesn't have any parents," Ben said as he made a show of blowing some smoke into the air.

My insides tightened into a knot. Ben was the only one I had ever confided in and shared my secret with. Would he...?

With a laugh that was more like a loud snort, Ben continued, "They gave him away. His mom and dad couldn't stand him!"

The betrayal made me feel sick to my stomach.

"Well, look at the creep," Ben went on. "He's so fat you'd think someone put stuffing into him. And that face full of pimples... Ugh!"

My arms were at my sides, hands balled into fists. I swallowed a huge lump in my throat. The air had become so still, not a breeze stirred. The group had closed into a circle around me.

"We need to beat the stuffing out of him!" Ben yelled.

Blinded by rage and fear, I caught Ben off guard as my right fist flew out and made contact with his nose. There was a sickening crunch of bone breaking and blood started streaming down his face. He grabbed at the front of his shirt and pulled it up to help stop the bleeding. Someone behind me gave me a shove and the others started toward me.

"Hey! Is that any way to treat my friend? The odds look a little uneven to me."

Warily lifting my gaze to the direction of the voice, I couldn't believe my eyes. Jerry sauntered up to the group, which automatically opened up and made way for him. He approached me, put his arm around my shoulders and said, "Will and I have an errand."

The group started to disperse. It was difficult to miss the looks of disbelief on several faces. My "good friend," Ben, was nowhere to be seen.

Jerry and I walked together in the direction of the gym. He didn't say a word, and I couldn't think of anything brilliant to break the silence. I was afraid I would say something stupid and he would turn on me, like the rest of them.

When we got to the rear of the gym building, he stopped, reached into his pocket, took out a kind of cigarette I had never seen before and lit it. When he blew out a stream of smoke, I couldn't believe the stench."Ugh! What's that? It reeks!"

Jerry chuckled and said, "Oh, this stuff will make you feel good. It's weed. Columbian Gold."

A Shattered Life Restored

Not being sure what that was, I just said, "Oh." After watching him for a couple of seconds, I blurted out, "Can I try some?"

He gave me a joint and watched. I inhaled and began coughing and gagging. After the initial shock to my lungs, and when the gagging subsided, I began to feel tingly and light all over. I liked it! After inhaling a couple more times, I was feeling better than I had ever felt before. It made me feel cool. There was this sensation that I could now do things better: walk better, talk better, hear better and love better. Colors were more brilliant. From that point on, I knew weed would influence my every activity. What I didn't realize is what a problem that would turn out to be.

As I lifted my gaze, I was startled by the almost evil glint in his steady, blue eyes as he watched me. Shadows of the tree leaves were dancing on the cement wall of the building and a cluster of them had arranged themselves behind his head, which made it appear he had small horns sprouting there. The corners of his mouth were turned up in a wicked-looking smile. When he spoke his voice was different, deeper, almost menacing. "Like it?"

"Yeah, it's great," I stammered, feeling a little ill at ease.

He chuckled, turned and started to walk away. "See ya around, kid."

My great new friend, Jerry, never sought me out again after that, but I went looking for him often so I could buy weed. It wouldn't be long before I realized that anyone who turns you onto drugs is definitely not a friend. I was 13 years old and a lifetime of addiction lay before me.

I never knew my mother. Later in life, I was told she ran away because she couldn't handle child rearing. My father was a truck driver, and although I believe he tried hard, he couldn't handle it either. He gave me to my grandfather and step-grandmother one day and drove off. I was 4 years old and I never saw him again.

When I was 7, my grandfather passed away and Grandma was faced with a tremendous decision. At 66 years of age, she could either accept the responsibility of raising me or send me down the road. She was a brave and courageous woman and she took me on. She had two elder sisters, Sally and Lucretia, who helped her out once in a while.

When I was 10 years old, I started working for my own money. I mowed lawns in the afternoon and on weekends, and I also had a paper route. Grandma adored me. She would do anything for me, and it was easy for me to manipulate her for money or anything else I wanted.

One Sunday morning, Grandma's sister, Sally, came barging into the house.

"Come on! We're all going to church." She was a Lutheran and she was always pressuring Grandma and me to go to church with her.

Sitting at the kitchen table, I raised my defiant gaze to meet hers. "I'm not going."

Grandma was at the kitchen sink rinsing off some of the breakfast dishes. Wiping her hands on a dishtowel, she turned to face me. "Will, let's go with Sally. You've never been to church and you need to know what it's all about."

My chair scraped loudly on the floor as I pushed myself away from the table and stood up. "There's no way I'm going, Grandma. There's nothing at church that I need to know about."

Her gaze met mine. There was a challenge in my eyes that usually worked to my benefit, but not this morning.

In a quiet, calm voice she said, "Go upstairs and change into your best clothes." She shifted her gaze to her sister. "How much time do we have, Sally?"

Sally glanced down at her watch. "Ten minutes and not a minute more." She looked triumphantly down her long, sharp nose at me as I flung myself out of the kitchen and stomped up the stairs.

St. John's Lutheran Church was a scary place to me. The brick building was huge, very ornate, cold and impersonal. It had cathedral ceilings, lots of stained glass windows and a pipe organ. The pastor and lay staff wore fancy, white robes with gold cords for sashes, there were lit candles all over the place, and there was a certain rhythm to the service that never changed. I hated it. It took up my whole Sunday. Being in church all Sunday morning and half the afternoon wasn't what life was all about for me. Somehow I ended up getting confirmed, and not long after that, I was able to worm my way out of going anymore by charming my grandma.

I did learn there was a God, but it wasn't a personal thing for me. On the other hand, I always had the feeling that God never left me. Throughout my high school years and into my early 20s, He sent messages to me.

In high school, I had a group of friends who were all stoners. One day, we were sitting around on a small, inconspicuous patch of grass at lunchtime, smoking weed, and a young man approached our group. He had blue eyes and blond hair, was dressed very nicely and he had a Bible with him. He didn't say "hi" or introduce himself in any way, but he started preaching from the Bible. I was lying on my side with my elbow bent so I could prop my head up with my hand. This gentle stranger, who wanted to preach to a group of tough-looking stoners, surprised me and when I heard the guy next to me start to snicker, I reached over and gave his shoulder a push.

"Hey! Knock it off," I whispered loudly. "Let's hear what he has to say." The group was feigning interest, but I found myself listening as attentively as I could in my drug-induced haze.

After about 15 minutes, he closed his Bible, smiled at us, turned and walked away. As soon as he was out of earshot a couple of the guys called out, "Jesus freak!"

After that initial visit, he came on a pretty regular basis. One day as we were all standing around, he looked right at me and said, "Have you noticed how blue the sky is today?" Tilting my head up, I lifted my gaze to see for myself and found he was right. In fact, it was so blue, it appeared to be glowing. A feeling of warmth and something like peace washed over me, and for a split second I was fascinated. When I lowered my gaze, he was gone. Instantly, I believed this young man knew we were stoned and that's why he came to preach to us. In my heart, I believed that was his "mission," to reach out to young people like us who were lost.

When I was 16, freedom came in the form of my first car. I went with some of my friends to a cabin at Dillon Beach on the California coast for a weekend of partying. The cabin belonged to the grandmother of one of the kids. We had arranged for a friend's older brother to buy us the booze we wanted. We also brought along some weed, a little bit of cocaine and some pills that were said to keep the party going, and we were sitting around inside, getting stoned.

"Hey, Will, pass me one of those beers. My throat is dry."

"Don't bother me, man. Can't you see I'm busy?" I had just started to snort a line of cocaine.

"Someone's knockin' on the door," Carl said. "Maybe it's the cops! Maybe we're busted!"

One of the guys peeked out a window close to the door. "It's two chicks! Shall we invite them in to party?" Everyone laughed and there were some lewd comments, accompanied by snickering.

"Man, don't get your hopes up," I said, as I got up and went to the front door.

Both of the girls said "hi" and asked if they could come in and talk with us.

"Uh, that's probably not a good idea," I said. Their faces were young, innocent and sweet.

They turned out to be Jehovah's Witnesses, and a few of the other guys came out on the porch with me and we talked with them for a little while.

Summer faded into fall, and winter came and went before the bunch of us would return to the cabin. Much to my surprise, there was a note tacked to the front door with my name on it. "Hi, Will. Sorry we missed you. Maybe we will catch you around. God bless." It was signed by the girls. Standing there with that note in my hand, I couldn't help thinking that I had had another messenger.

From my sophomore year in high school until early adulthood, I learned all there was to know about drugs and the partying lifestyle. I experimented with just about anything that came my way, including LSD, mushrooms, PCP, angel dust, heroin, cocaine and crank. By the time I was 21, I was hopelessly lost in addiction and spending every dollar I made on drugs and alcohol. When I couldn't get drugs from regular sources, I would take to the streets and solicit the services of hookers on the strip because they always knew where to find good dope. One night, I decided I wanted to smoke some crack, so I hooked up with this gal who took me down a dark driveway, knocked on the window and this guy looked out.

"Yeah? What do you want?" Then he noticed me. "Who's that?" He came running outside with a large caliber handgun.

"Down on your knees, pig!" Turning aside to look at the girl, he said, "Is he a cop?" Before she could answer, he turned back to me and gave me a vicious kick, then planted the gun into my neck. The cold, deadly metal pushed into my flesh and I started to cry.

"Please don't kill me," I begged.

"Yeah! Yeah! That's what I want! Beg me not to kill you!"

I was so terrified all I could do was stammer and stutter. "P-P-Please d-d-on't kill me."

The gal who brought me there yelled at this guy. "Stop! Stop it! Look at him! He's scared! You've made your point! You've done enough!"

He slammed me on the back of the head with the butt of the gun, but it didn't knock me out.

"Take off and never come back!" he screamed, as I scrambled up to my feet. Both the girl and I ran back to the car. The first thing I did as soon as I got home was smoke some weed so I could calm down. That was the last time I tried to get crack cocaine. It was also another message, but the more stoned I got, the easier it was to brush it off.

After coming to my senses, I realized that the streets were packed full of trouble, so I gave up getting drugs from unknown sources and only bought from people I could trust. When first introduced to me, methamphetamine was known as the "poor man's" cocaine. It was cheap, easy to get and lasted much longer. I decided to try meth primarily for economic reasons. It didn't take me long to become what some experts would call an industrial or functional user, and it soon got to the point where I needed the stuff just to be able to function. Some people want their coffee first thing in the morning. I wanted a line of dope.

My routine was to party all weekend and use meth so I could stay up the whole time. The first time I did this, when Monday rolled around, I had to go to work, but I felt sick. I had a tiny bit of meth left over from the weekend. *I'll use this last little bit to see what happens.* It perked me up. It made me feel good again. I went to work, came home and crashed. When I got up the next day and got sick, I didn't have any of the stuff. I had to contact a guy who did.

"The only way to feel better is just use the stuff, but don't go overboard." That was his advice.

Well, this stuff costs money. Most of my hard-earned cash was spent on drugs and partying, and when the money was gone, I needed to find ways to come up with more to buy it. I started taking some of my personal possessions to the pawnshop, my TV, a handgun, etc. Then I would get a loan on whatever I pawned. The problem with that was I started to be late on my loans.

Now I found myself in the downward spiral of an addict. I started losing my possessions. When I started losing stuff, I stopped paying my bills. The next thing I knew, I didn't have a telephone, I didn't have any lights, and the landlord was knocking on the door for the rent. When the money and valuable possessions ran out, I resorted to criminal activity to fill the void. I did this six times in my life. Each time, I had to start with nothing and build my life back up again. Slowly but surely, I then started taking it apart, brick by brick, until I had nothing left. At that point, although I really didn't know God, I prayed to Him anyway. "God, would You bless my mess?" I lived like this for the next 18 years or so.

When I was about 27, I met a woman. Until then, I had never had an actual girlfriend. I had always been awkward with girls because my self-esteem was very low and I feared rejection. When I met Laura, I was bartending in Sacramento. My self-esteem was at an all-time high. I was flying high on drugs and I was tanned and thin. Things were going well for me. I had money and a car, and I was doing drugs all the time.

Hot Mama's was a neighborhood bar that offered food as well as booze. It was housed in an old, brick train depot building. Etched into the brick over the front door was the year "1895." Inside it had an old plank floor that I thought could easily have been the original. The walls were covered with black and white photos of old trains. The chandeliers were old wagon wheels with fake candles. Batteries provided the "flames." The air was a blend of greasy food, stale cigarette smoke and alcohol. The roar of several blenders accompanied the clink-clank of ice cubes used for certain mixed drinks.

Standing at the bar, wiping out the inside of a glass,

A Shattered Life Restored

I happened to glance up in time to spot a cute, young thing stepping over the threshold with a friend of hers. She looked to be about 20 years old, and as soon as she saw me, she steered a course toward me. She found an empty stool and perched on it with her friend occupying the one next to her. I put a basket of salsa and chips in front of them. "What can I get for you ladies?"

"I'll have a gin and tonic," she purred.

I was attracted to her, so I decided to serve her.

As I turned to her friend, I saw her stuff a chip into her mouth and salsa slithered off and dripped down the front of her blouse.

"Oh... I'll be right back, Laura. Gotta get some water on this before it settles." And with that, she slid off the stool and headed to the ladies' room.

The jukebox came to life and I turned my attention back to Laura. She hung around until it was time for me to close up. Her friend never returned. We went to Laura's place and partied, got high on meth and booze and started a relationship, just like that.

One day, she started begging me to take her out of California on a vacation.

"Please, Will. I haven't been *anywhere*." We were sitting side by side on the couch. She ran her fingernails lightly down my cheek while she blew in my ear.

"Honey, I haven't been any further away than Oregon." I laughed as I removed her fingers from my face and held her hand.

"But that's great! Can we go? Let's go, Will!"

"Okay, okay. I have some vacation time coming to me."

We planned to leave two weeks later, and I borrowed a van from one of my friends. We camped at various places, both along the way and inside Oregon. I was more in love with her than she was with me, and that became painfully clear the night we broke up in Oregon. We were in a bar and she started talking to this young college kid who had come on the scene. He was good looking, had an athletic build and was very interested in Laura. I sat there brooding, feeling like a fifth wheel, when she spoke to me.

"Will, we need to go outside and talk."

"Why outside?"

"I have something to tell you and I can't do it in here."

My stomach tightened with anxiety, and I slumped over the bar with my head down for a few seconds before I slid off the stool. Her face looked pinched and a little pale. When we got outside, she gave me the news.

"Will, I've decided to stay here in Oregon."

"What do you mean?"

"I mean I want to stay."

"It's that guy at the bar, isn't it?"

"Well... yes. Don and I want to be together."

My heart was broken. We had been together for one and a half years, and I didn't want to believe she would dump me, just like that. It was very hard for me to take that rejection, but I knew what would fix me up.

Giving her a last look, I headed for the van and started back to Sacramento. I used meth, got high and stayed high all the way home.

The gloom and despair of depression overwhelmed me, but I was determined to turn my luck around. Being a recent graduate from radio school, I took off for a job in South Lake Tahoe at a small radio station. "Sin City" offered all the gambling, prostitution and drugs anyone could want and I became a party animal. Working the night shift meant that I got off work at 6 a.m. A cab driver friend and I would then pick up girls that had been in the casino all night and party with them. I got deeper and deeper into drugs.

During the holiday season, Laura called me. "Will, he's been beating up on me!" I was still nuts about her. "I still love you, Will." I fell for that, hook, line and sinker, because that's what I wanted to hear. We got back together, and within a couple of months, she discovered she was pregnant. Both of us tried to straighten up our lives. She had the baby. It was a boy and we named him Kevin. We had been living with my grandma for about a year when Laura told me she wanted to leave. She had always blamed me for her problems, and she said having the baby had ruined her life. One of her girlfriends was moving to Colorado with her boyfriend. "I'm moving to Colorado and I'll be back in a month for the baby. If you don't like it, you don't have to come."

Three weeks later, I packed up everything I had, including Kevin, who was about 16 months old. We took off for Colorado. My friend, meth, was with me all the way from California to Colorado. Laura and I resolved our problems and tried to straighten up our lives. I worked two jobs just to try to get ahead, and by the time I got home at night, I was exhausted and ready for some relaxation. One night, I came home early and found her cheating on me with one of my drug dealers. That was it. She had made the final cut. Dealing with all the drugs, whining and complaining were things I could handle, but being unfaithful? To me, that was an abomination and I couldn't tolerate it.

"Remember when you told me you wanted your freedom?"

Her eyes were huge and her gaze was fixed on mine.

"Well, you got it, babe!" I went into Kevin's bedroom, scooped him up, and we left for Sacramento. He was almost 4 years old. I never heard from Laura again.

When we got back to Sacramento, I was determined to make changes in my life. No more drugs and alcohol. No more being taken advantage of by temporary "friends" and the drugs they had. I got help training for a new career and began working as a tow truck driver. At least in this field the likelihood of me getting high and working was slim to none, or so I thought.

After a few months of being out of the party scene, an old friend of mine re-introduced me to meth. I was working 24-hour shifts on call, and crank was the one thing I knew that would keep me alert in the wee hours of the morning. Before I knew it, I was on my way to being on the stuff all the time. However, I managed to keep my drug use hidden, told myself that it wasn't "that bad," and I would quit when I didn't need to stay awake all night.

One Friday afternoon during the summer, the temperature reached 104 degrees. I had been driving the tow truck all day without any air conditioning. Glancing down at my watch, I saw I only had 30 minutes to go and I would be off work. My idea was to start heading in that direction and I would pull into the lot right about 5 p.m. "Just as long as I don't get a call..." I hummed to myself. Sure enough, I got a call and I was 15 miles away from her location. "Swell! Go all the way across town at 4:30 in the afternoon on a Friday. She might as well walk because she will get wherever faster!" It was a "car won't start" call, and I was supposed to tow it back to Rio Linda, which was another 40 minutes from where it was broken down. I was boiling mad! I wouldn't be able to party until 7:30 or later.

When I reached the location, I could clearly see both the car and the woman. She was waving her arms and doing what we call "The Triple A Shuffle," trying to get my attention. She didn't think I saw her. Just to be mean, I drove around the parking lot pretending that I didn't see her, but I could only get away with that for a couple of minutes. Pulling up beside her, I got out of my truck and started talking to her about her car problem. I couldn't help noticing that she was cute and had a nice smile. She was wearing a little summer dress. As I was talking to her and writing down information on the service ticket, I suddenly said, "Ma'am, you sure have pretty legs." She flushed crimson from the top of her head to her bare shoulders.

She started to get into the cab of the tow truck. There was no way I could help her without putting my hands in inappropriate places. "Can you manage it okay?" I asked.

She paused on the step while she held onto the handgrip, turned her head and looked down at me. "Yes, I'm fine." Her eyes were as brown as milk chocolate, and they were soft and sweet. The sun danced on her wavy, red-brown hair, causing it to shimmer with glittering highlights.

I caught my breath and thought, *Could I be falling in love?*

We took off in the direction of Rio Linda and chatted a bit about her car problem. Without even stopping to think about it, I said, "How would you like to stop for a bite to eat?" I glanced down at my wrist and checked my watch. I didn't have much time before I needed to get back with the tow truck, but I decided to spare about 40 minutes.

"That would be fine. I'd like that."

Yesssss! I was pleasantly surprised that she accepted.

We stopped at a little place where they used to sell produce that had been converted into a small, rustic restaurant. Inside, the stone walls were white and cool. There was a small bar in the back, a stone fireplace on one side and a large salad bar on the other. The lighting was dim. We found a booth and sat opposite each other. Our waitress appeared wearing a red and white gingham apron over jeans and a white t-shirt. She was chewing gum with her mouth open and it snapped and cracked as she said, "May I get you something to drink?"

Overcome with awkwardness, I didn't know what to say. I lifted my gaze and met Jaclynn's. "Would you like a beer or something?"

"Actually, I would love a beer."

Far out! We have something in common. Turning to the waitress, I said, "We'll have two Coors on tap."

"Comin' right up." She quickly disappeared.

My body was leaning in toward the table, my hands clasped in front of me. "So, Jaclynn. Tell me a little bit about yourself."

"Nothing much to tell, Will."

"You know my name? How'd you know that?"

She smiled as she pointed to my chest area. "It's embroidered on your work shirt."

Stupid! I felt so stupid! I had forgotten all about that. My face flushed and I knew I was pretty red. We both broke out laughing and that really broke the ice.

The waitress returned with our beers. "You folks ready?"

"Two burgers with everything and some fries." I looked over at Jaclynn with my eyebrows raised as if to ask, *Is this fine with you?*

She read my look and said, "That sounds good." As we ate and drank our beer, she started to talk. "Well, I'm a single mom. I have two kids. My daughter, Jessica, is going to be 7 in a couple of weeks, and Matthew, my son, is 4."

Almost choking on a bite of burger, I replied, "Amazing! My boy, Kevin, is 4." *How great this is,* I thought. *Her kids are about the same age as my Kevin. Hmm. This could be good.*

We finished our meal with some small talk. I didn't have much time to linger. We walked up to the register together, Jaclynn went outside to wait for me, and I put some bills on the ticket and left. We were pretty close to where she lived, so within 10 minutes, I had dropped her off.

From then on we were dating. A couple of weeks later it was her daughter's birthday, so I bought a little, blue dress thinking I would score some points with Mom and I did. We formed a relationship, but neither one of us knew that the other did drugs. We drank beer together and had a good time. We built the relationship on that.

Kevin and I moved into Jaclynn's apartment after the third date. One day the following week, she had a doctor appointment and said she would be gone for a while. After about 10 minutes of twiddling my thumbs, I decided to smoke some meth. I sat around the place, smoking, until about 30 minutes before she had told me she expected to return. I was busy doing those fidgety things tweakers do when she returned.

"Hi," she said casually, as she laid her car keys on the small table by the front door.

"You're back."

She had a peculiar, sort of wondering look on her face. "What's that smell?"

"What smell?"

"Oh, come on. I'm not stupid. I know what dope smells like when you smoke it."

"You do?"

We stood there silently appraising each other. We had just found out each other's dirty, little secret. As far as I was concerned it was great because, in addition to our beer drinking, we could use drugs together. I said, "I didn't know you used."

"Yeah, for several years. How about you?"

"A long time."

That night was the first time we got high together.

Eventually we moved into a bigger apartment, and finally, we rented a big house in Rio Linda near her mom's house. We were both fully into doing drugs, and I had a very good job with the Freeway Service Patrol. It was a state-funded job where tow trucks would patrol the freeways during rush hours and help people for free if they had any trouble.

Jaclynn and I were together for five years when the meth started breaking down our relationship. We both got paranoid, jealous and started doing things we didn't ordinarily do. As for me, I was out with other women, sharing dope and having affairs. Jaclynn was out partying all the time.

A Shattered Life Restored

Around 2 one morning, after being at the strip clubs, I tried to quietly let myself into the house in the hope I wouldn't wake her.

When I opened the front door, the light from the street lamp across the road spread a shaft of light into the room. Jaclynn was sitting on the couch smoking. With the other hand, she was swirling the liquid from some kind of drink around and around very slowly in a glass. She took a deep drag on her cigarette and said, "Where have you been?"

"Well, I had a late tow and then..." I was stammering as I frantically ransacked my brain to come up with something believable.

She gave a short, hard laugh. "Oh really, Will. Surely you can do better than that." She knocked the ash from her cigarette into a tray on the table beside the couch and took a swallow of her drink as she waited for my response.

When nothing was forthcoming, she stubbed out her cigarette, put her glass down on the table and stood up. "Let me rephrase. Who were you sleeping with to-night?"

Trying to stab her back, I said, "Must you always be so suspicious? Maybe I had mechanical trouble. Maybe some of the guys and I stopped off for a few snorts. Maybe..."

"You're a liar! At least be man enough to tell me the truth!"

The tension between us was palpable. We were both glaring at each other in that shaft of light. I finally slammed the door as hard as I could and made my way to the bedroom. Jaclynn never came to bed with me that night.

Financially things were going downhill too, and we moved to a smaller house in Citrus Heights. We were messing up big time. I was using more than I had ever used. I used it to wake up. I used it later in the morning. I used it on coffee breaks and during lunch. Jaclynn was using as much as I was. We were fighting, picking at each other all the time and couldn't agree on anything.

One afternoon, Jaclynn got so high she grabbed a kitchen knife from the drawer. She didn't try to stab me, but she did go outside and threaten to slash the tires on my tow truck. That would have really been bad for me because I didn't own the truck.

"Maybe if I take your precious wheels away, you won't be able to spend so much time with your hussies," she hissed at me. Then she started screaming and making wild, slashing movements in the air. I was afraid to make any kind of move. She ran into the house and called the police. "You'd better get over here right away and pick me up or someone is going to get hurt." They came and took her off to the local psych ward for a 72-hour watch.

When Jaclynn called me on my cell phone and said it was time for me to pick her up, I was trying to buy some dope from a gal and, well, doing something else with her that I shouldn't. We had run out of booze and I happened to be at a 7-Eleven store, right across the street from her apartment. It had a very distinctive bell over the door, and Jaclynn was familiar with both the store and where Brandy lived. On the phone, I lied to her. "I'm on a tow, babe."

"No, you're not! You're at Brandy's place!"

We had a big fight, she grabbed her kids and took

off for Oregon where her sister lived.

Kevin and I were alone. He was older now and needed a stable family with responsible parents. And I had a really bad drug habit. We found shelter on the sofas of drug dealers and acquaintances. In some ways, having a young boy was an advantage for a homeless man, but in others, it was devastating. When our welcome ran out, I sought the services of the Welfare Department. At least there we could get a motel room for the night. My life was rapidly sinking. Once, I even broke into a house while the woman who lived there was at work so that Kevin and I could clean up a bit. All the while, it never occurred to me that meth was the reason my life was falling apart.

One day several months later, my phone rang. It was Jaclynn. Feelings of surprise and delight washed over me. I missed her terribly, but I wouldn't tell her that. I was barely hanging onto my tow truck job and I was trying to tell her all the dumb options I had when she said, "Well, the door's always open up here if you ever need it."

We talked back and forth for a couple of days. It was around Christmas time and our hearts were softening. For the first time, we both admitted we had lots of flaws. We made an agreement that I would come to Oregon as a "friend." On January 1, 1999, I arrived. Before long, we were back together. We agreed that we would drink only, and maybe smoke a little bit of weed, but that's it. We both insisted meth would no longer be a part of our lives.

I got a job as a tow truck driver the very next day. It didn't take long for dope to come back into the picture. We thought we could control it; we thought we would only do it a little bit. That didn't work. My problem got worse and worse, and my attitude was affected so badly that the tow truck company fired me.

Back on the pavement looking for work, I knew I had to clean myself up a little bit. Pre-employment drug tests were always a possibility. I lucked out and started working at a radio station. We fell in with the "cool people," and we became pretty popular ourselves. We were doing so much dope and were so out of control, it wasn't long before the cops came to the door and busted me for receiving stolen property (which I traded for dope).

In June 2001, I told my boss at the radio station that I was going on vacation. The truth was I had no intention of ever coming back. Jaclynn and the three kids had gone ahead of me to Sacramento. It was pretty well planned out. We lived in tents in her mom's backyard and when the money ran out, I had to get a day labor job. Jaclynn's mom was already established in a church and had been saved several months before we arrived. As a new Christian, she started talking "that talk" to Jaclynn and somehow convinced her to go with her to Fair Oaks Open Bible Church.

When Jaclynn came home from church that first Sunday, she said, "Hey, I think you will like it. They have music there that you like, guitars and stuff."

My mind turned that over a few times. "Well, sure. Anything is worth checking out. If nothing else, it might be entertaining." I went and I actually kind of liked it. I remembered church as a place where they used hymnals, played the organ and that kind of stuff. When I heard the band and praise and worship team do "Awesome God" in that church, I said, "This isn't like any church I've ever seen!"

July turned into August and the pastor, Duane Coller, stood up one Sunday morning and said in a powerful voice, "Are you running from the law? Are you addicted to drugs? Are you lying? Are you cheating?" He paused, and you could have heard a pin drop. Leaning forward on the pulpit, he pointed his forefinger out at the congregation and almost whispered, "Is it well with your soul?" Talk about getting my attention! There were at least 200 people in the congregation, but I felt like he was just talking to me. Everything he talked about in that sermon was a mirror of my life. While he was speaking, he and I made direct eye contact a number of times. It was very intense. The Holy Spirit had moved over me and I felt convicted.

That sermon shattered my foundation. Later, I would learn that it did the same thing to Jaclynn and her mom. The Sunday after the sermon, some of the men in the church started to work on me. They invited me to go to San Jose, California, to a conference in September called "The Promise Keepers."

"Nah. Not interested, too churchy for me. Besides, you guys are Christian men. Even though I have been rattled a little bit by today's sermon, I'm not doing a two-day event with a bunch of guys I don't even know."

One morning in September, my clock radio went off loudly and startled me out of a deep sleep. It was 5:30 a.m. and the date was September 11, 2001. It caught my attention immediately.

"Ladies and gentlemen, a plane has just crashed into the World Trade Center!"

At that time, I was working as a maintenance man at a trailer park, and I had to get up and go to work. As the

171

events of 9/11 unfolded, I watched a little bit on TV, and in my very clouded and distorted mind, I thought, *Oh, how fascinating.* To me it was a neat event, not a disaster. I went to work and spent all morning inside the tool shed, listening to the radio and getting the latest disaster news from New York City. It suddenly dawned on me, as I was smoking bowl after bowl of meth, that I wasn't feeling anything for these people. There were witnesses on the radio who were crying, describing the horrific destruction and chaos, and I couldn't even feel sad for them. I was more concerned that I was going to run out of dope soon, and I wasn't sure where I was going to get more.

The invitation to the Promise Keepers Conference kept turning around in my mind, and I started feeling a strong desire to attend that. It was on Friday and Saturday, September 14th and 15th, and I decided to go. Stuffing some weed in my pocket, I took off.

Friday night, I was sitting in the audience and watched a man drag a giant log into the San Jose arena and up onto the main stage. There was an axe up there, and he started chopping away a little bit at the log. He started telling a story while he was chopping.

"I wonder what life was like for the man who made the cross they used to crucify Jesus." Chop, grunt, chop, grunt. "Did he know the King of Kings was going to die?" Chop, grunt, chop, grunt. This guy was truly laboring as he chopped. He was breathing hard and had to stop and catch his breath every so often. He had to wipe the streams of sweat that were running down his face. "What if Jesus were to be crucified on a cross that I made? Oh, God!"

Then it just hit me! He was actually making a cross

A Shattered Life Restored

out of that log. I was very shaken.

Saturday, as I was sitting on the edge of my bed in my room waiting for the morning session to start, I smoked my last half joint. That was the last time I did drugs.

The conference started with praise and worship. The arena holds 15,000 people and it was filled to the brim with men. Words to songs they were singing were up on a screen, and I was singing along and going with the flow, when the words to the next song were put up. The song was "Amazing Grace." All my life, I had loved that song. For some reason, it was very close to my heart.

At first the singing was soft and tender (*Amazing Grace),* but as more and more voices joined in, there was a swelling of music that soared to the heavens above (*how sweet the sound),* a tremendous chorus of men's voices so strong I thought I could feel the ground tremble under my feet - *that saved a wretch like me!* It took my breath away.

The sound of more than 15,000 men singing Amazing Grace without any instruments accompanying them, just their voices, gave me goose bumps all over my flesh. The inside of that arena just resonated and the sound shook the place. My throat closed up and for the first time in years, tears began to fall from my eyes. I began to tremble. *Why can't I sing this song? I love this song!*

A man on the stage directed everyone to find paper and pencil and start writing down their sins. I ripped a page out of my program book, someone gave me a pencil and I started feverishly writing. Some of the things I wrote were: "I am a drug addict. I have stolen. I have

173

lied. I have cheated." The man on the stage asked us to come down and put our lists of sins on the stage. I didn't know what was happening to me. I was trembling and crying as I made my way to the stage.

On the way down, I heard him say, "Come on! You have a chance to get forgiveness. God is here and He wants to forgive you." As soon as I put my list on the stage, I fell to my knees. I was praying the sinner's prayer and a group of men surrounded me and laid hands on me. When I finally walked back to my seat, I felt I was somewhere outside myself, all upside down and topsy-turvy with emotions.

As I sat down, I saw some conference workers on the stage. They were stapling all the lists of sins to the cross that the other man had chopped out of that log. There were thousands of pieces of paper.

At the end of the conference the most beautiful thing happened. They rolled six or seven dumpsters onto the stage, tore the sin lists from the cross and threw them into the trash, a symbolic gesture that indicated, "You are totally forgiven now!" That was the day I turned my life over to God.

God's forgiving heart didn't stop there. "He who began a good work in you will continue to do so until the day of Christ Jesus." (Phil. 1:6)

Driving to church alone one Sunday morning, I sagged with an unexpected burden on my heart. The power of the Holy Spirit overwhelmed me with another message. *Stop running! Turn around! Come back home to the One who created you, according to His greater purpose.*

God asked Jaclynn and I to make things right in our lives, and that included going back to Oregon to face up to our mistakes. This wasn't going to be easy, but we knew it was something we had to do. Two weeks after the conference, we packed everything up and went back. Turning myself in was tough, but after I was booked into the jail, I was immediately released and they set up a court date. Jaclynn and I checked ourselves into rehab right away. When my court date rolled around, I was sentenced, but *something* influenced the judge to keep me out of jail. In my heart, I believed that God was responsible for that.

Jaclynn and I were married in July, 2002. Just when I thought God had done a great work with us and changed our lives for good, He showered me with His grace yet again when I got my radio job back. In addition to being the News Director, I am the Chairman of the Jefferson County Methamphetamine Task Force. In order to be sure my soul stays in tune with God, I bought a guitar so I can sing praises to His name.

Now instead of doing drugs, I seize every opportunity to write articles, produce radio programs and talk to school kids and church groups about the dangers of a life on drugs. Praise God that I am finally beginning to understand why I was allowed to be a drug addict for so long. The Bible teaches us about this. James 1:2-4 says, "My Brothers and Sisters, when troubles come your way, consider it an opportunity for great joy! For you know that when your faith is tested, your endurance has a chance to grow. So let it grow, for when your endurance is fully developed, you will be strong in character and ready for anything." No longer do I depend on drugs and the evil devices of our eternal enemy's influence. Life is so much better with God than without!

Afterword

Amazing Journeys

I'm sure you enjoyed reading these stories, and I pray that these pages have ignited hope in your heart. The miracle of Christ working in the heart of faith is, without a doubt, the most life-changing experience any individual can undergo. We are convinced God designed people to live in a community where they can be encouraged, strengthened and honored. A community where questions can be answered, people can be given time to contemplate and where loving one another is the greatest joy.

You are invited to come and visit our church. Come and meet the people whose stories you have read. Come and meet many more people with similar stories. Come and join in this great adventure of living life with a completely different focus and a truly unlimited resource.

We open our doors to you, extending hands and hearts in your joyous welcome.

Finally, if you would like to meet this Jesus who has done so many things in our lives, please call and let us visit with you. You can also consider the following and then pray the prayer at the end. Either way, we do encourage you to give us a call and let us share your joy and walk together.

Recognize that you are dying because of your sin.

Rom 6:23: "Work hard for sin your whole life and your pension is death. But God's gift is real life, eternal life, delivered by Jesus, our Master." THE MESSAGE

Believe that God, your Father, loves you and wishes to give you a new heart.

Ezek 11:19: "I will give them singleness of heart and put a new spirit within them. I will take away their hearts of stone and give them tender hearts instead..."

Afterword

NLT

Believe that God, your Father, wishes to fill your new heart with His life.

2 Cor 5:17: "What this means is that those who become Christians become new persons. They are not the same anymore, for the old life is gone. A new life has begun!" NLT

Believe that God, your Father, can transform your whole life through Jesus Christ.

Eph 4:22-24: " ... take on an entirely new way of life — a God-fashioned life, 23 a life renewed from the inside, 24 and working itself into your conduct as God accurately reproduces His character in you."

THE MESSAGE

Prayer:

Lord Jesus, I recognize that my sin is killing me physically, emotionally and spiritually. I need You to give me a new heart so that Your life can come and fill me. I recognize I am a sinner and need to be forgiven so I can escape the judgment of loss of life. I believe Your blood has forgiven my sin and I receive Your forgiveness. I welcome Your Holy Spirit into my new heart. I give myself to You so You can begin to remake and transform me. Amen.

Lee McCloud

Living Hope Christian Center

Madras, Oregon

We would love for you to visit!

Please stop by Sunday morning, we're located at 25 NE A St. P.O. Box 707 on the South-East corner of NE 5th and NW A St. Or for directions, call the church office at

(541) 475-2405

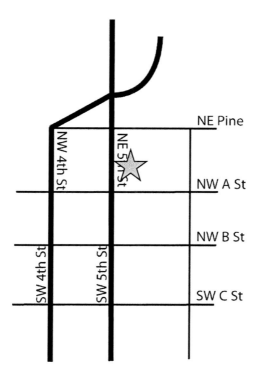

We would love to hear how this book has impacted your life! Please write us at info@livinghopecc.com
Or visit our website at www.livinghopecc.com

For more information on reaching your city with
stories from your church, please contact
Good Catch Publishing at
www.goodcatchpublishing.com

GOOD CATCH
PUBLISHING